S0-ARE-874

HELPING YOU IS HELPING ME

Virgil Crittan

Helping You Is Helping Me

*How a New Breed of Volunteers
Can Make a Difference*

Virgil Gulker

with

Ken Wilson

Servant Publications
Ann Arbor, Michigan

Copyright © 1993 by World Vision, Inc.
All rights reserved.

At times the names and characterizations in this book are
fictional, although based on real events. Any similarity
between the names and characterizations and real people
is unintended and purely coincidental.

Vine Books is an imprint of Servant Publications
especially designed to serve Evangelical Christians.

Published by Servant Publications
P.O. Box 8617
Ann Arbor, Michigan

Cover design by Steve Eames

93 94 95 96 97 10 9 8 7 6 5 4 3 2 1

Printed in the United States of America

ISBN 0-89283-807-8

Library of Congress Cataloging-in-Publication Data

Gulker, Virgil.
    Helping you is helping me : how a new breed of volunteers
can make a difference / Virgil Gulker, with Ken Wilson.
        238 p. cm
    Includes bibliographical references.
    ISBN 0-89283-807-8
    1. Voluntarism—United States. 2. Volunteers—United
States. 3. Social service—United States. I. Wilson, Ken, 1952–
II. Title.
HN90.V64G85   1993
361.3'7—dc20   93-19425

Dedication

For my wife, Kathy, and our daughters,
Emily and Laura.
You are the helpers in my life.

NOTE TO THE READER

At points in the text, the author and co-author use the first-person singular as the narrative voice without specifying who is speaking. However, usually the speaker is the author. Further, most of the personal illustrations and examples are the author's; but occasionally, they are those of the co-author.

Contents

Acknowledgments

So MANY PEOPLE have made contributions to *Helping You Is Helping Me.* Let me tell you about some of these wonderful people.

Ken Wilson, my co-author and a talented writer, crafted words that communicate compassion and helped to popularize my material for today's reader.

Mary Tuinsma, my gifted office manager, provided invaluable research and word processing services. Equally important, she shared insight and encouragement at every stage of the book's development.

Karen Gullett helped in outlining and researching the material in this book.

Dave Came and the other folks at Servant Publications were always available to provide direction and encouragement.

Many volunteer agency directors have generously shared their insights and the experience of the volunteers and the clients they serve. National, regional, state, and local leaders in two exemplary federal programs—Head Start, and the Special Supplemental Food Program for Women, Infants, and Children (WIC)—have given me an invaluable opportunity to link church volunteers with disadvantaged children and their families. Some of their experiences are included in this book. The Points of Light Foundation shared their list of Volunteer Centers, which is provided in Appendix One of this book.

Last and most importantly, I want to thank the millions of volunteers who are helping people in need. They are the heroes of this book and the hope of our troubled land of America.

ONE

The New Volunteer

Dateline—May 3, 1992: The volunteers poured out onto the angry streets of south central Los Angeles only hours after the violence had subsided. They appeared almost as if by magic amidst the rubble and burned-out shops and apartment buildings. A city and a nation that had turned away in shame and fear after the explosion of rage over the Rodney King verdict now turned back with a measure of surprise and hope to see hundreds of people on the city's sidewalks and streets. Unlike the rioters, these people did not tote guns, knives, and firebombs, nor were they intent on revenge.

These volunteers were young and old, urban and suburban, individuals and families, rich and poor, students and professionals, residents and illegal aliens, some of whom knew no English and had cowered in their apartments for days without food, electricity, or water. Broadly representative of the diverse economic, ethnic, and generational threads which make up the colorful social fabric of the city, these compassionate citizens remained anonymous good Samaritans. Many came with brooms and shovels to clear away the debris. All of them came with a desire to help rebuild lives and neighborhoods shattered by the worst urban riots in modern American history.

Crisis situations have always helped people bridge their differences. Neighbors may be powerless to avoid most disasters. But in the aftermath of disasters, these same neighbors—even neighbors who may never have spoken to each other—will rally together in a work of rebuilding and restoration.

I remember a little girl who was helping her mother in a Los Angeles church pour rice into small plastic bags for distribution to families in need. Her face beamed with pride when I thanked her for helping her neighbors. She and all of the children who volunteered for this marvelous work of restoration may never forget the ugliness of the riots. Yet they will certainly remember that their response to hatred and revenge was love and helping. They were a light in a very dark time.

Sadly, the empowerment and community involvement which followed in the wake of the riots dissipated within days. When the appropriate response was no longer clearly defined— visiting neighbors in need, sweeping sidewalks and streets, escorting the injured and sick to clinics, comforting the victims, and so much more—the volunteers simply left.

Many of them still wanted to make a difference. But the authorities told them that even though they had done a good job of cleaning up, now the really important work of rebuilding the community was to begin. It was time for the volunteers to step aside and let federal, state, and local organizations take over. Thank you very much. You may go home now.

Imagine that! Just when the really important work begins, the volunteers are told that their work has come to an end. And if anyone doubts the ability of government agencies to rebuild broken lives and devastated neighborhoods, visit Newark where city blocks destroyed by riots years ago have yet to be rebuilt. Or visit Los Angeles where the frustrated director of the city's rebuilding effort blames his lack of progress on the failure of government, at all levels, to deliver.

The tragic story of massive urban violence was limited to the inner city of Los Angeles in 1992. Yet the potential for more social unrest simmers just below the surface in other urban areas. The Los Angeles riots can be seen as a paradigm or model of sorts for America on two levels. First, our country is being torn apart by the same kind of prolonged economic and racial tensions that contributed to the rage in Los Angeles. Second, and more importantly for our purposes, the people who helped in the aftermath of the riots represent a promising new breed of volunteers.

These people were prepared to participate directly in the re-building of their neighbors' lives. They weren't content to wait for the appropriate government agency to arrive on the scene. Instead, they began, almost immediately, to make a difference in the lives of real people in need in their community.

Let me share a more personal example of this new breed of volunteer—one that is unrelated to the Los Angeles experience and could easily have occurred in just about any community across America.

It began with a grocery bag that seemed out of place. Christopher, an appliance repairman for the laundromat, saw that it didn't seem to belong to anyone. When he looked inside, he found a wallet, a birth certificate, a job application from McDonald's, and a diary.

Christopher soon realized the young woman pictured on the driver's license was in trouble. Obviously in need of a job, she had no personal identification. Like a detective searching for a missing person, he made a few phone calls from the bits of information available.

Before long the owner of the lost items began to take on a name and a face. A rough outline of her story emerged. Here was a nineteen-year-old running away from an abusive family situation, her father already in prison. Christopher and his fiancée, Mary, thought about giving all the information to the local police, but how much attention would the already over-loaded department give to another case in the missing persons' file? To Christopher and Mary, she was becoming, if not a friend, at least a neighbor. Her name was Ann.

So they traced Ann to the waiting room of a local hospital.

It turns out that a hospital waiting room is a good place to stay for a few nights until the hospital staff catches on. Clean, warm —and free coffee. Ann was thrilled to have her wallet and other important papers back. Perhaps she could get that job at Mc-Donald's now. Mary offered to take Ann shopping for some fresh clothes. More thankful than embarrassed, Ann agreed that might be a real help.

Christopher, working through his church, arranged to provide Ann with temporary housing through a house for homeless women. He and Mary kept in touch with Ann until she moved out of town—back on her feet again.

I never met Ann, but I talked with Christopher and Mary several times during their experience of helping Ann. They were literally thrilled with the opportunity to actually make a difference in one homeless person's life. Their helping was no mere drudgery—the joyless fulfillment of a civic obligation. It had an invigorating effect on this engaged couple. They discovered what thousands of others have discovered in the act of helping others: helping you is helping me.

Christopher and his fiancée had never worked in a soup kitchen, never served in a homeless shelter, never volunteered to be a big brother or sister, never even given blood. Like countless thousands of Americans in the 1990s they had an itch to help, but they didn't know how or where to begin. Stuffing envelopes for a charitable organization wasn't their idea of making a difference.

The endless statistics quantifying the needs of the homeless, the elderly, and the poor intimidated Christopher and Mary as much as they intimidate most of us. What can one person accomplish in the face of such overwhelming need? Joining Mother Teresa's Missionaries of Charity was out of the question. Yet they knew that the simple deeds of love shown to those in need are at the heart of biblical faith. And like so many of us, they had a desire to make a real difference.

President Clinton, in his 1993 inaugural address, called on

all Americans to "take more responsibility, not only for our-selves and our families, but for our communities and our coun-try.... It is time to break the bad habit of expecting something for nothing, from our government or from each other." He challenged "a new generation of young Americans to a season of service—to act on your idealism by helping troubled chil-dren, keeping company with those in need, resurrecting our torn communities. There is so much to be done, enough for millions of others who are young in spirit to give of themselves in service, too."

"In serving," the President continued, "we recognize a simple but powerful truth—we need each other. And we must care for one another. Today, we do more than celebrate America; we dedicate ourselves to the very idea of America."

A QUIET REVOLUTION IN PROGRESS

Chris and Mary and the volunteers in Los Angeles exemplify what may yet become a revolution in the way we think about helping neighbors in need. They capture in their actions the spirit of President Clinton's challenge to America. For decades, we've paid our taxes, contributed to United Way and the local soup kitchen, hoping that the social service experts would take care of these problems. We've tried welfare, work-fare, learn-fare, and a host of other programs. We've poured more money into programs, tried to reform them, and better coordinate them.

We're learning the hard way that the society that relegates the needs of its neighbors to systems and institutions eventually cuts them off from the people who can actually help them. The system is not the solution. Government assistance plays an important role, but nothing can replace love personally deliv-ered to a neighbor in need. This is the primary value shared by the new volunteers.

People like a woman from Seattle whom I'll call Odessa

Riley are demonstrating that one person can make a difference. Mrs. Riley wasn't sure what she could do to help the struggling kids in the local elementary school. Join a committee? Run for the school board? Volunteer to be a crossing guard? Nothing seemed to fit. Then Mrs. Riley's daughter reminded her how much the hugs she had received every morning before school had meant to her, hugs that a lot of the kids at the school were missing.

So Grandma Riley, with the support of the principal, stationed herself at the entrance of the school each morning, to greet each child, parent, and teacher and offer Grandma hugs to all. Only a few refused. Before long, people were talking about the difference Mrs. Riley was making in the morale of the school. Mrs. Riley is not alone.

Even the program directors of the welfare system are beginning to realize that money and expertise cannot compare with the power of an ordinary person who puts a name and a face on poverty and helps a neighbor in need. Bob Vernon, the former assistant commissioner of police for the city of Los Angeles, underscored the power of the human touch when he told me, "I'd almost rather see a successful volunteer program come into Los Angeles than for the city to receive more and more federal money. I've been a police officer here for thirty-six years. I've seen so much federal money go down a rathole. If we can link only four hundred church members with four hundred people in need, we can begin to change Los Angeles. A caring person helping another person in need is very dynamic. Both are changed for the better."

The former director of the federal government's Supplemental Nutrition Program for Women, Infants and Children recently told me that the churches could impact a whole generation by reducing infant mortality, low birth weight, and developmental disabilities, thereby reducing the drain on our already overworked health care system.

"How much would that cost?" I asked, excited by the possibilities for his proposal but anxious about the price tag.

"Nothing," the program director replied.

"All we need are experienced moms and grandmothers who can put their arm around one pregnant woman, tell her about the value of breastfeeding, and help her get to a clinic for regular check ups. That's all it would take."

David Hollister, a state senator from Michigan and a long-time welfare proponent, recently said, "The private volunteer groups have now become the safety net in our society. Even if the economy improves tomorrow, the welfare system will never again be the primary care provider."[1] This represents a major shift in perspective. Had you suggested this in the 1970s to Senator Hollister he would have certainly denied it.

What the people who make their living running government programs are saying is, "We need people more than money." Could they be right? Is that really all it would take? Sure, money is important. But we've overestimated what money can buy. The crippling problems facing our country are not yielding to money. We need people helping people, one person at a time. An approach that recognizes this simple truth could lead to a revolution in the way we take care of our neighbors in need.

PEOPLE WANT TO HELP

And by all accounts, more and more individuals are convinced it's worth a try. According to a 1990 study, volunteering in the United States increased 23 percent over the previous two years. More than 98 million adults are giving over 20 billion hours of their time.[2]

In Indianapolis, LOVE INC, an organization dedicated to matching the needs of individuals with a person (not just an agency) who can help, asked the members of four churches (1,460 individuals in all) to volunteer to help people with specific needs. In other words, they were not asked to raise funds for an organization, or give two hours per week to an agency, but to help an elderly gentleman stay out of a nursing home by buying groceries for him, or to help a single mom keep her old car running.

How many church members were interested enough to sign up? I would have been impressed to see 10 percent respond. I was amazed when 1,263 individuals offered themselves.

People want to help their neighbors in need. You want to help. Otherwise you wouldn't pick up a book like this. So I would like to make you, the reader, a few promises.

WHAT YOU DON'T NEED

First of all, you don't need a scolding. I will assume that you are the kind of person with a sincere interest in making a difference. You want to help. Therefore, I have no interest in motivating you with stern lectures meant to make you feel guilty. I've heard presentations of pressing social needs that imply that you and I are responsible for the estimated 100 thousand homeless children, or the 12.6 million children who live in poverty, or the multitudes suffering from AIDS.

You are not personally responsible for these staggering numbers. But you are interested in helping a homeless child, or helping a single mother take some steps toward getting out of debt, or helping to care for a man with AIDS. My challenge is to help you put a name and a face on these problems; to help you find a child like Juanita, Sichor, Billy, or Tabitha, and get involved in a way that really makes a difference.

There's something else you don't need: a course in statistics. I will do my level best not to overwhelm you with numbers in an effort to shake you out of some presumed middle-class lethargy. We've all heard the statistics and they usually just send us scurrying for cover. We're convinced already that the world is going to hell in a hand basket, and at a faster rate than when we last checked. We don't need to be persuaded about the needs. We want to get on with helping.

YOU ARE THE CUSTOMER

This book is not written for any agency or organization seeking to fill a quota of volunteers. You're the customer, not some organization trying to cut their personnel costs. I've spent seventeen years recruiting and training volunteers to work with people served by private and public organizations. I've volunteered my own time to many different groups. I know there are plenty of volunteer opportunities that are frankly not worth filling.

Indeed, while I support President Clinton's plan to develop a national volunteer service plan, I frankly doubt the capacity of existing organizations to use these new volunteers in meaningful ways. The needs are there, but many organizations are not able to handle more volunteers. Other service agencies don't use volunteers at all.

All this means that there are traps to be avoided when you give your time to help others. I've fallen into most of them myself. I once volunteered for an agency seeking to help needy people. I pictured being a "big brother" to a young boy, or distributing food to those in need. Instead, the volunteers met before Thanksgiving and Christmas to pack food baskets. The baskets were then delivered by agency staff so that the volunteers "would not have to be involved." But to be involved was my reason for volunteering in the first place. I hope to help you avoid some of the traps that discourage people from lending a hand to a neighbor in need.

This book is written for you, the person who wants to help someone in need, part of a new breed of volunteers. I'm committed to helping you make the most of your time which, I'll assume, is what you are interested in, and not a scheme to pass the time of day or to help you cut down on an addiction to soap operas. You have plenty of things to do with your time, but helping people is important to you.

There are strategies to help you make the most of your time. Like you, I want your investment in helping others to actually make a difference in someone's life. I think of Elizabeth who volunteered to assist in her church's mission to "help the widows and orphans." She eagerly participated in preparing a care package for a widowed woman from church whom she had never met. Elizabeth even volunteered to visit this person each week to ease her loneliness. Imagine Elizabeth's amazement, which soon became embarrassment, when the volunteer group visited the widow's home and it turned out to be one of the most exclusive addresses in town. The widow was not a regular churchgoer because she was frequently travelling abroad!

Happily, Elizabeth's next volunteer experience was much more profitable. She agreed to participate in a literacy program, working with Thanh, a Vietnamese refugee and mother of four who needed to learn English in order to pass the citizenship test. Elizabeth was trained by the program in the best methods of tutoring Asian adults. In the process of tutoring, Thanh learned to read and Elizabeth and Thanh developed a good friendship. This is the kind of experience I want you to have.

HELPING YOU IS HELPING ME

Exciting new research is confirming something that should not be surprising: It seems that loving your neighbor is at least as good for you as it is for your neighbor. One study suggests that people who volunteer actually live longer than those who don't. Another researcher speaks of a short-term and long-term phenomenon called "helper's high."

An investment banker in Southern California was deeply troubled by the tendency of his influential elderly friends to turn to drugs and alcohol soon after retirement. Almost tongue in cheek, he suggested a unique solution for them that could also solve my organization's need for funds: charge these retirees fifty dollars per hour for the opportunity to mentor a child. Not a bad idea. This banker knows that helping you is indeed helping me.

Ask anyone who has taken the plunge to share his or her most memorable experience in helping other people. The stories will vary, but you will hear a generous sprinkling of comments like, "I received more than I gave." By learning how to make the most of your volunteer investment and how to avoid some of the common pitfalls, you will reap more of the built-in benefits of loving your neighbor. And that's good for everyone, because it will keep you in the game.

PUTTING FEET ON FAITH

A large percentage of those who volunteer to help others are motivated by their faith. They are frustrated with a church or synagogue that is little more than a social club or a religious society. I've learned that most people who are serious about their faith need realistic opportunities to express the heart of God toward those in need more than they need browbeating from the pulpit. For too long, the church has taken a back seat to the bureaucracies of the state when it comes to helping people in need. We make our contributions to keep the church running and pay our taxes to help the poor. But in the coming years, those motivated to put their faith into action will become a major force again in ministering to the sick, the prisoners, and the poor.

Ruth Mary is part of a congregation in the Los Angeles area not far from a women's jail. She noticed many of the women who were released from the jail had a common set of needs: new underwear, a nice hair cut and styling, and a clean outfit for a job interview. So many of the women seemed to have lost their dignity along with their clean record.

That bothered Ruth Mary, so she and some of her friends at church converted a portion of the church building into a boutique—a place for women to come after being released from jail to meet some other women and get a fresh start. The women who staff the boutique find a natural setting in which to befriend someone who could use their help. They are meeting real needs and having meaningful contact with the people in need; and it's not frightening, awkward, or embarrassing for anyone.

YOU CAN MAKE A DIFFERENCE

If you're like me, the most powerful fear you face when you think about lending a hand to a neighbor in need is not, "Can I spare the time or the energy?" Your biggest concern is not, "Will I get ripped off in the process?" More than anything else, you wonder whether you really have what it takes to make a meaningful difference.

Like the rest of us, perhaps you've been influenced by the cult of the expert. You probably imagine that those most effective in helping others are people with incredible relational skills, years of training, extraordinary talents, and possibly a few letters after their name.

A funny thing happened on the way to the psychiatrist's office. The experts have discovered the limits of their expertise. There is growing controversy over how effective psychotherapies really are in helping people resolve personal problems.[3] I'm not suggesting we shun professional counseling. In many cases, professional counseling is required. I'm just suggesting that those in the helping profession don't have a corner on the helping market.

So this book is not about becoming an expert or a hero. It's for ordinary people like you and me—people who want to make a difference and just need a little help to get started.

TWO

The Hidden Benefits
of Helping

Whext WE CONSIDER THE POSSIBILITY of volunteering time and energy to help someone in need, we often focus exclusively on the benefits to the person helped. The homeless woman, the man with AIDS, the boy in high school with no father to guide him. But anyone who spends time helping others knows that there are powerful benefits to the person doing the helping.

Why are 98 million Americans giving more than 20 billion hours of their time every year? Why is Peter Drucker, writing in the Wall Street Journal, projecting that within ten years the ranks of volunteers will swell to 120 million, a full two-thirds of American adults? Certainly not because people find themselves with more free time than ever before.

Through firsthand experience we are learning that everyone wins when we invest time and energy to help others in need—the person helped, but no less, the person helping. It pays to love your neighbor. In their recent book, *The Healing Power of Doing Good*,[1] Allan Luks and Peggy Payne document the "health and spiritual benefits of helping others."

Why are more and more employers encouraging, even requiring, their employees to spend a few hours each week in volunteer work? In one Chrysler plant, two thousand employees take one hour a week to help elementary school students understand better the relationship between what they are learning in school and the marketplace. At Duke Power, located in Charlotte, North Carolina, 2,300 employees volunteer as tutors, mentors, and guest teachers.[2]

Sure, it's good public relations helping a company establish a reputation for caring that goes beyond the profit motive. And business leaders are realizing that a good business environment requires more volunteer investment to help young people become productive contributors to the future labor force.

But there is also a growing recognition that employees who volunteer their time to help others tap into a wide range of hidden benefits themselves. They learn new skills. They feel better about themselves. They are motivated by a sense of purpose beyond simply doing their jobs. They gain new perspective on their own lives. And all this makes them better people, better employees. We all win when we love our neighbors as ourselves.

Just ask one of those 98 million American volunteers like Rose who wanted to sharpen her Spanish skills by helping a little Hispanic boy learn English. After tutoring nine-year-old Jose for a year, Rose realized that her volunteering gave her more than an opportunity to keep up her Spanish.

"You get addicted to this. I feel I get at least as much out of it as the kids do. These kids bring so much to your life. Sometimes because they learn something, and sometimes just because of who they are," says Rose.

In fact, one study, conducted in Tecumseh, Michigan, suggests that volunteering to help others may even play a part in lengthening your life. After following 2,700 men for ten years, the researchers found that those who volunteered their time lived significantly longer than those who did not.[3]

Jumping into a volunteer activity is a little like beginning to exercise. For most of us, exercise doesn't come as easily as, say, stopping for ice cream. There are benefits, to be sure, but the benefits are not all short-term, and they are to a certain extent hidden until we stick with it for a while. Sometimes we begin to exercise for one reason—perhaps to lose a little weight— only to find many other benefits awaiting us.

For example, I didn't get serious about exercise until I was literally forced to when I ran into that brick wall called burnout. I had so little energy and motivation for life that I was desperate to try anything—even exercise. So I began to jog and work out with a few exercise machines.

Over time, my energy level did increase, but by then I had discovered firsthand other benefits to exercise that I hadn't anticipated. There was that immediate feeling of well-being after a vigorous run that comes with the release of natural endorphins, chemicals that deaden pain and literally help us to feel good. I had read about that, but feeling it was another thing.

I also started to feel better about myself. I had gotten used to a poorly conditioned body, one that was in gradual decline. But when I began to tone up my muscles and actually gain strength, my self-esteem grew stronger too.

By focusing on the hidden benefits of helping, I am not suggesting that giving your time and energy to help others in need is a simple matter of enlightened self-interest. Without question, the people who are most likely to give of themselves in various volunteer efforts have deeper motivations than this. They are not helping simply to feel good, meet other people, or improve a resumé.

People who volunteer give three times as much money to charitable organizations as those who do not. Those who attend church tend to volunteer more than those who do not. Of those who attend church weekly, 56 percent volunteer. Of those who never attend, 33 percent volunteer. The spiritual values stressed in a church setting obviously provide powerful motivation for people to help other people.

These hidden benefits of helping may not provide the most

powerful reasons for volunteering, but they are real benefits nonetheless. God has designed built-in rewards for loving service to others. It's good for those served and good for those serving.

What are some of those hidden benefits that await us as we give time and energy to help others through some regular volunteer activity?

Maximizing Your Health Benefits

We need the right help, not just any helping will do. For maximum health benefits, you must select the best volunteer activity available. Here are some guidelines:

- *Personal contact.* Spending time with people has a more lasting effect than impersonal tasks, such as collecting clothes and food for the poor.
- *Frequency.* Helping at least two hours a week is enough to spark changes in your life.
- *Work with strangers.* Assisting strangers is more powerful than helping family and friends because there is no feeling of obligation as there is with family and friends.
- *Effort.* Like exercise, the best results are achieved when volunteers have to exert themselves.
- *A shared problem.* A feeling of bonding and the reduction of stress are more pronounced when a volunteer has something in common with the person being helped.
- *A supportive organization.* It offers a more powerful sense of teamwork and connection with other helpers than does working alone.
- *The use of skills.* An activity that matches a volunteer's abilities is likely to produce the most positive experience.
- *Ability to let go of the results.* Forget any benefits you might expect to give or receive; just enjoy the closeness you feel with those you're helping.[4]

1. Volunteers get a kick out of helping others. Rose talked about "getting addicted" to her volunteer activity. Many volunteers echo her words. There's just something about helping others that literally helps us to feel good. Allan Luks, executive director of the Institute for the Advancement of Health, describes this as "helper's high." He described feelings reported by volunteers in *Psychology Today*, October 1988.[5] Over 700 of those polled reported one of more of the following sensations while volunteering:

Feeling "high" 52%
Feeling "stronger, more energetic" 44%
Feeling "calmer, less depressed" 25%
Feeling "a greater feeling of self worth" 21%
Feeling "fewer aches and pains" 14%

According to another study, "Several volunteers described the sensations they felt from helping to be similar to those they got playing sports. Unlike sports, however, most volunteers surveyed said their sensations would recur when they recalled the helping experience."[6]

A good example of this is African-American police officers in Houston who have volunteered to mentor and tutor young children in inner city schools. For the officers, when they recall their experience, they say it was much more than just a chance to help a child. It was an opportunity to show the youngsters, many of whom distrust the police, that police officers are people, too. They are people who have families and people who care about kids. The officers feel good about sending that message.

2. Volunteers gain a sense of impact or significance not always available through career or other responsibilities. Marlene had spent the past ten years of her life raising four children. She was a stay-at-home-mom who supplemented the family income through a small tailoring business. While her family responsibilities provided a deep satisfaction, there was something missing in her experience of life. Marlene was a nurturing person and good with her hands, but there was also an assertive side to her personality that thrived on a good debate and the challenge of moving immovable obstacles for a good cause. In the best sense of the term, Marlene was a fighter. She would have made a good politician or trial lawyer.

Of course I didn't realize that Marlene was a fighter until she took on the one-sided social agenda being promoted in the local school curriculum. Until that time, Marlene always struck me as a talented person who had never quite found her niche in church. She's found her niche now through her active involvement in the politics of education. She's brought a new sense of sanity into the curriculum of the local high school, worked hard to elect school board members who are supportive of her values, and is currently bringing her gifts to bear on her daughter's private school.

Marlene is experiencing one of the hidden benefits of volunteering. She has a new sense of impact—the satisfaction that comes with making a difference in the world.

We all have a longing for impact, a deep-seated desire to make a difference, to have our lives count for something beyond ourselves. There is more to life than earning a living, doing our jobs, and caring for our families. Volunteering even a few hours a week to help others in need can provide a wonderful opportunity to make a real difference.

During this era of economic retrenchment, many are realizing that the workplace doesn't satisfy this longing to have an impact. With diminished job opportunities, people are less satisfied with their lives on the job. When asked in a Harris Survey whether the quality of life at work among six thousand office workers was improving, the percentage of respondents saying yes followed this pattern:

1978	70%
1986	56%
1988	55%
1989	55%
1991	44%[7]

Volunteering a few hours a week to help someone in need can provide a much needed sense of accomplishment, not always available through our jobs. Yes, volunteers face challenges, but they are different challenges than the ones we face at work. The rewards are different too.

Don, who organized a mentoring program for African-American elementary school students, matching adults with disadvantaged students to give them one-on-one attention, told me recently: "I'm forty-eight years old and I've never felt so good in my life. I've had men say to me that they can die now because they've accomplished something." Volunteering provides us with that opportunity—to accomplish something, to make a real difference in another person's life—not necessarily through the sharing of high-level skills, but more often than not by making some time available and simply "being there" for someone.

3. Volunteering enhances employability. A quick look at the employment section of the newspaper reveals that most employers are looking for people with experience. For the person with little work experience—a young person entering the work force or a homemaker re-entering the work force after working at home for many years—this is a real catch-22. No job without experience, and no experience without a job.

Volunteering provides the side benefit of valuable experience, enhancing employability. If you volunteer for an organization or agency, often someone within the organization will be responsible to oversee your work. In most cases, you will provide invaluable help, and your contribution will be appreciated. Your supervisor will be an excellent reference for future jobs. If this is an objective in your volunteering, it would be wise to select an organization or activity that provides direct supervision.

You will also have the opportunity to meet other people who appreciate your work. They may be fellow volunteers, people you help, or their relatives and friends. Some may be businessmen and women who could use someone with your abilities. The more people who appreciate your contributions and know you personally, the broader your network of potential references or even employers.

Does this sound a bit too self-serving? Don't worry, most

Volunteering Your Way into a New Career

If you are thinking about volunteering to help establish yourself in another career, here are some tips from Michael Falk, director of program services at the Volunteer Center, Orange County West, California.

1. Plan to have a backup job or alternate source of income. Changing careers through volunteering will take at least a year of your time.
2. Start by volunteering a few hours a week. Don't commit too many hours before you know you can handle it and that you like the volunteer work.
3. If you need to work during the day, be aware that there are many evening and weekend volunteer opportunities.
4. Be flexible. Don't be afraid to try more than one volunteer assignment until you find one you like. Be willing to try new tasks and activities.
5. List your ten most valuable skills and be prepared to share them with a volunteer coordinator.
6. Form a mental picture of the role you would like to play. What skills do you hope to use? What new skills do you hope to learn? What kind of people do you see yourself working with?
7. Continue to explore other pathways, besides volunteering, toward a new career. Don't put all of your eggs in one basket.
8. If you want to work for a nonprofit organization, start by volunteering. It's the best way to get your foot in the door.[8]

volunteers find ample opportunity for genuine sacrifice and self-giving in their volunteer experience! You won't be wanting for chances to put the interests of others above your own.

4. Volunteering helps you discover what color your parachute is. For those entering the work force or considering a change in career direction, it is important to learn what your interests and strengths really are—a process one vocational expert calls "discovering the color of your parachute."[9]

Volunteering provides an excellent opportunity for field-testing your interests and discovering abilities you never knew you had. Sue was a stay-at-home mom for eighteen years, caring for five children. She began to feel a strong sense of compassion for women facing problem pregnancies. The only groups offering solutions in her town were the abortion clinics, and that didn't seem right to Sue. "We need to do more than oppose abortion. Someone needs to help these women with crisis pregnancies!"

Sue was not formally trained in one of the helping professions, but she was a mother of five children with a wealth of experience and practical know-how. Maybe she could help. As she shared her vision of a clinic to help women facing pregnancy in difficult circumstances, she discovered others with a similar passion. Before she knew it, Sue was involved in launching what would become the Pregnancy Counseling Center, serving women with crisis pregnancies.

At first, Sue gave her time as a planner, phone caller, and organizer. Once the clinic was open for business, she worked directly with pregnant women and was thrilled to have a hand in helping a mother choose life for her child. In the process, Sue discovered that she was good at what she did. Eventually she went back to college, obtained a professional degree in social work, and found herself with a new career now that the children were older. For Sue, volunteering to help others in need provided the catalyst for discovering abilities she hadn't recognized before, and a pathway to reenter the career marketplace.

In a 1992 Gallup Poll for the independent sector, 58 percent of teenagers, ages 14-17, had done volunteer work in the previous twelve months. They are smart kids because volunteering is an excellent way for young people to discover what color their parachute is. Many teenagers have a variety of untested interests. They change majors in college every other semester, it seems, searching for a satisfying direction. Talking with a nineteen-year-old named Maja about her career choices helped me appreciate the benefits of volunteering.

Maja was among the 58 percent who volunteered. Though interested in a people-oriented career, she felt that hospital nursing was not one of them after a summer spent volunteering at the local hospital. She had field-tested her interest in nursing and realized it wasn't for her. This young woman had also given two weeks of her summer helping in a orphanage in Honduras, was a camp counselor, and worked as a "big sister" in a youth program—all excellent experiences for discovering her interests and abilities.

5. Volunteering helps turn negative life experiences into strengths. Joe led what is sometimes mistakenly called a "colorful life" as a young man. He landed in jail for the possession and sale of cocaine. After his release from prison, Joe's life turned around as a result of a profound religious conversion. As he puts it, "I met Jesus, and he fixed me like I could never fix myself." Ordinarily a criminal record is a weight that must be carried throughout a person's life. It is for Joe. But through his work with prisoners in a local jail ministry, Joe has turned his negative experience into an advantage. Joe understands the struggles that prisoners go through—the loneliness, the despair. And he is not easily conned by an inmate who decides to play games with him. He can see through that in a minute. All this makes Joe a highly effective volunteer. He's good at what he does.

Sarah spent two years in a deep depression. With the help of professional counseling, she was able to trace her depression to two abortions she had had as a younger woman. As she faced the grief and tragedy of her own experience and received the forgiveness and grace of a compassionate God, Sarah's depression eventually lifted. After a few years, Sarah discovered that she was able to help other women facing abortion because of her own experience. She didn't have to imagine what it must be like. She knew. And she was able to speak to the concerns of these women with conviction and authority. She was able to cry with them and help them face up to difficult choices.

Perhaps the outstanding need of people in tough circumstances is for someone to talk to. The need isn't so much for advice as it is for someone who will listen with real understanding. And few people are able to listen better to someone in need than someone who has been there. So when you consider how you might be able to help others, don't simply think about what you're good at, but what you've been through. Don't just count up what you view as strengths but consider your failures too because they may hold the key to your effectiveness in helping others.

The Twelve Steps of Alcoholics Anonymous incorporate this concept in the twelfth step of recovery which insists on the need for recovering alcoholics to help their fellow alcoholics recover.

For the recovering alcoholic, reaching out to other alcoholics is not simply a good deed, though it is that. It is part of his or her own recovery.

6. Volunteering can provide a break from preoccupation with your own problems. People who volunteer their time to benefit others will often report that the experience helps them gain perspective on their own lives. It is an opportunity to move beyond our natural tendency to be preoccupied with our own problems. Volunteer experiences encourage us to come out of ourselves, an experience many people find to be refreshing.

Because our society is inundated with advertisements for a variety of new, expensive products, we can easily slip into a vague sense of dissatisfaction with what we have. The car we're driving can never compare with the cars hugging the scenic drives on the television ads. But as we step out and have real contact with people less fortunate than ourselves, our whole frame of reference—our sense of reality, our view of the world—is adjusted, and we begin to focus on what we have more than on what we lack.

Melinda is a case in point. She is a young woman with multiple sclerosis who longed for an opportunity to help people as a volunteer. Yet most organizations treated her as a client rather than as a resource person. Finally, she was given an opportunity to use her gifts. She became the volunteer "playlady" in the waiting area of a public health department. She cares for the small children while their pregnant mothers are receiving check-ups. Melinda is now valued by others and is making a real difference. She also feels good about herself and is less preoccupied with her own problems.

Or consider the extraordinary experience of some veterans who were staying at a San Diego hospital after losing arms and legs in the Vietnam war. Each of the men had fallen into such a state of deep depression that they were unable to communicate with anyone.

The nurse who cared for these men tried everything to coax them out of their depression. Finally, she realized that their injuries had robbed them of any meaningful sense of impact. No one was counting on these men for anything. And they were suffering for it.

The nurse brought several terminally ill babies, who had no contact with their parents, from the pediatric floor into her ward. She appealed to the men for help: "These babies are dying. But they have no one to love them and bond with them. They need you."

Those babies began to work a miracle in the minds and hearts of the battle scarred veterans. The babies were secured to the chests of the veterans. They couldn't be ignored. The gentle pressure on their chests was a constant reminder to the men. They were needed. They looked into the tiny eyes of a baby gazing back at them, or peered with wonder at the peaceful face of a baby asleep, or heard the cry of a baby in distress.

Within days, all the disabled veterans had escaped their depression. They were actually orchestrating the care of the babies, talking to them, singing, ensuring that they were fed and changed. That part of them that was truly human, that was designed to have an impact, to be needed by someone else, was reawakened.

7. Volunteering provides an advanced degree in the school of life. Those who volunteer to serve others frequently tell of invaluable lessons they've learned from people they help. A friend of mine visits terminally ill patients at home who are receiving hospice care. He once quoted to me an obscure passage from the book of Ecclesiastes, "The heart of the wise is found in the house of mourning."

"I never understood that," he told me, "until I visited people who were facing death. For example, the terminally ill have taught me a lot about what really matters. Have you ever tried to buy a birthday present for someone who has only a short time to live? Material possessions don't have much appeal to those who are dying. People, relationships, love, settling conflicts—those are the things that matter to them. And it is very powerful when they speak of the things they regret in their lives: missed opportunities, petty grievances. I often come away from time with a dying person feeling that I've received as much as I've given."

Another volunteer named Ethelyn tells of working together with Rob, a young man with AIDS who came to her church in search of acceptance and a place to be able to help others. He gave time to the benevolence ministry of the church which reaches out to poor individuals. Ethelyn said, "I'd been a member of this church for fifty years, but I learned so much from Rob about suffering, about peace and patience."

There was a time in my life when I thought that I possessed more answers than questions. This was roughly the same time that I despaired of my parents ever really knowing anything or understanding me. I believed, for example, that I understood various social problems because I had researched them as part of my academic training. Then I met some of the people who were part of the "problem" and I realized that I did not understand the things I had studied very well at all.

I thought I understood prostitution until two prostitutes—Margharet and Dorothy—volunteered to assist me in developing a paperback library for the women in a Miami jail.

I thought I understood capital punishment until three killers —Walter, Harold, and Joey—whose sentences had been commuted, stepped forward to help me offer college-level courses for inmates at the Attica Correctional Facility.

I assumed that I understood child abuse until I counseled and assisted Hal and Myra, Ben and Sally, and other parents who had abused their children.

I thought I understood nursing homes until staff members and the family members of residents at a home implored me to file charges against the management for flagrant abuses.

I thought I knew a little about Alzheimer's Disease until I screamed at my own mother in a moment of overwhelming frustration and rage.

YOU CAN'T OUTGIVE GOD

These examples of the hidden benefits of helping others simply illustrate that you can't outgive God. It's a foundational principle of giving summed up in the proverb, "A generous man will prosper; and he who refreshes others will himself be refreshed" (Prv 11:25).

Jesus stressed the same point when he said, "Give, and it will be given to you. A good measure, pressed down, shaken together and running over, will be poured into your lap" (Lk 6:38). There are built-in rewards to helping other people, hidden benefits. They can't always be predicted or controlled like the return on a certificate of deposit. But they are very real.

THREE

Looking Beyond the Need to See My Neighbor

I MET BILL ON A PLANE departing from Chicago. He had survived the loss of his bankrupt business and was finally getting back on top. But the bankruptcy had frightened him and he needed to tell his story. After completing his blow-by-blow account of his economic roller coaster, Bill felt obliged to ask about my line of work. That was his first mistake.

I told Bill about my efforts to mobilize church volunteers to get involved in the lives of the poor. Especially children. Abused children. Forgotten children. The children of children, who have no one to love, protect, or nurture them.

Bill peppered me with questions about my work and about the kids. Then he paused. "I drive through south Los Angeles day after day. And I see the children there, sometimes playing on the overpasses as I cruise down the freeway. I want so much to do something to help those kids. If only I could. But what could I do?"

Though Bill saw children in need every day, he saw them from a great distance. They were a blur along a busy freeway, a part of the urban landscape. Their paths crossed but their worlds never intersected. After another long pause, Bill asked again, "Is there a way I could help those children?"

"Yes," I replied, "there is a way you can help those children —by helping one of them." Even as I answered Bill's question, I knew that it would take a whole new way of looking at people in need before Bill would actually believe that he could do something to help.

Whether he knows it or not, Bill has been trained in a way of thinking about people in need that makes it difficult to do what isn't really that difficult—to reach out and lend a hand. It's as if invisible walls have been built up that prevent many of us from making contact with people in need. These walls keep us from looking at people in need as neighbors.

The section of Los Angeles that Bill passed through every day on the way to work would later become the epicenter for the Los Angeles riots of 1992. I am convinced that the despair that made Los Angeles so vulnerable to the riots will not be alleviated with money alone, or even with a more enlightened urban policy. It will take a revolution in the way we think about people in need—a new mentality that sees the people behind the needs, along with a new hope that is willing to invest in a person-to-person strategy. Only then will people like Bill, who represent a vast but untapped resource, be able to lend a hand to their neighbors in need.

BREAKING THE ANONYMITY HABIT

Most of us in the modern world are trained to keep other people at a distance. We spend so much of our time in crowds that we learn ways of shutting people out. We get unsolicited phone calls from perfect strangers asking us for money, or worse, we get up from the dinner table to answer a call from a computer! No wonder we feel a need for a protective shell.

Early on we learn to move through life with a shield of anonymity. When you step into an elevator with other people, there seems to be an unwritten rule observed by everyone: Don't make eye contact and don't say a word. So we stare at the changing floor numbers above the elevator doors as if transfixed.

A few decades ago, we knew the people in our neighborhoods. But now we have neighborhoods without neighbors. Maybe we should call them "strangerhoods." Before the advent of television, people hung out on their front porches and neighbors caught up on the latest gossip. But the eerie blue light behind the curtains changed all that. Now we build decks in our backyards and don't fuss much with front porches. Many people are not even able to name the people who live next door, a few apartments down, or across the street. When I lived in a large apartment complex in Miami in 1972, I wasn't aware that Angela Davis, one of the FBI's most wanted fugitives, was living in one of those apartments. Neither was the FBI, apparently.

Occasionally, this invisible boundary of anonymity is broken, and it is most uncomfortable. A stranger approaches us on the street asking for spare change. Sometimes we pay him off with a couple of quarters; sometimes we pretend not to notice him. But always, we feel uncomfortable, ill-equipped, awkward, wondering if our contribution will really help or just go for a bottle of cheap wine.

As the needs in our society increase, our ability to keep a distance from human need is taxed. Nancy, a volunteer at a soup kitchen for the homeless, was serving food to the nameless faces who passed her station on the serving line. She had been trained to look into the faces of those she served. But for Nancy, this simple task so vital to protecting the dignity of the people served was painfully difficult. Try as she might, she could not lift her eyes from the plate.

"I must do this," Nancy told herself, resolving to look into the face of the very next person she served. Nancy looked up and saw her own sister, Linda, waiting for her portion of mashed potatoes! Here she was, not a stranger, not a nameless face, but Nancy's own flesh and blood.

Yes, problems like homelessness are coming closer to home for many Americans. In January 1992, a Time/CBS poll indicated that six in ten Americans say they are encountering the homeless in their own communities or on their way to work rather than simply learning about them through the media. Only six years earlier, most Americans—six of ten—only knew of homelessness through media reports.[1]

These encounters violate that invisible boundary with which we surround ourselves. They fray the cloak of anonymity which protects us from the unwanted intrusions of people we have not invited into our world. It presses the point: What will we do—find ways of helping or hunker down and build higher and thicker walls?

THE WAR ON POVERTY: SOMEBODY ELSE'S BATTLE

In the 1960s Michael Harrington wrote a highly influential book on poverty titled, *The Other America*.[2] He described the invisibility of the American poor, isolated in rural areas or concentrated in inner-city slums few people visited. Their plight was further disguised by the availability of inexpensive but good-looking clothing.

The American Government, supported by a public eager to eradicate poverty, launched the War on Poverty. Unfortunately some of the methods of that campaign had unintended consequences. By placing the stress on creating agencies to dispense government funds rather than focusing on the need to build relationships between the haves and the have-nots, the poor were further isolated. The presence of a burgeoning bureaucracy to meet the needs of the poor gave everyone the impression that someone was taking care of the problems of the poor. We contracted out our good deeds to professionals. We felt we were doing our part by paying taxes. But this was more illusion than reality.

The welfare model is focused more on particular needs than on helping people as people. There are many who work within our public welfare system who care very deeply for the people they serve. But the welfare system betrays their love and concern by focusing not on the person but on the need. The welfare system is concerned with dispensing stipends, vouchers, food stamps. In other words, welfare tends to focus on commodities, not individuals. The welfare institutions are designed to provide short-term assistance to alleviate a need temporarily. They were never designed to provide someone with the kind of support a person needs to succeed.

Gregg Petersmeyer, an advisor to former President Bush, spoke recently of the limitation of the welfare model to provide the kind of help people need:

> We are faced with a handful of issues that are running out of control. They cry out for the building of one-to-one relationships. If today is normal, 3,700 high school students will drop out of school and never go back, and 2,600 unmarried teenagers will become pregnant on a normal day—children having children. These are good people free falling through American society because they are living in communities which have disintegrated. There are tens of millions of individuals who wake up in America and go through their day without one person caring about what they think or did. They live in abject aloneness from God or from those around them. It is literally impossible for them to develop a sense of individual worth.[3]

The welfare model alone—giving money or food stamps through an impersonal institution—doesn't touch this kind of need. What's needed? A person who cares befriending another person who is lonely. It takes people, often working with established government programs, to do that. This fact became clear to me when I talked with the Head Start Director in North Lawndale, a Chicago neighborhood that has lost forty thousand manufacturing jobs in fifteen years. What helps did this

Director want for mothers in need? She requested volunteers for three tasks: teaching the mothers to sew, how to dress for a job interview, and how to fix a running toilet.

Mothers living in Detroit's devastated Woodward Corridor asked for similar helps in an overall plan of "getting back to basics." They wanted help in particular with literacy and speaking skills so they would feel comfortable talking to their children's teachers.

STATISTICAL OVERLOAD

Our preoccupation with statistics has created another wall, keeping us from viewing people in need as neighbors. Virtually every news report chronicles the statistics of need. A recent news broadcast I watched indicated the percentage of people unemployed and the latest statistic from the World Health Organization estimating the number of people infected with the AIDS virus. A typical night's news.

Taken as a whole, this preoccupation with statistics tends to paralyze us. After all, what can any one person do to stem such a tide? Somehow the statistics cover up the fact that behind every number is a name and a face—a real person with a real need. Categories and percentages seem beyond our grasp, but individuals can be helped.

The War on Poverty generated a host of social scientists adept at slinging statistics, emphasizing data and trends, pointing to sweeping solutions based on complex analyses that barely seemed within the reach of a national government, let alone an individual. The experts were approaching the problem from the perspective of their own disciplines, which are helpful and necessary. But this approach did not help us put a human face on need. Rarely did their analysis or recommended measures boil down to what you and I might do to help a young single mother struggling to raise two children while training for a better job.

The generation of baby boomers (those born between 1946 and 1964) have been raised with this statistical view of people in need. The War on Poverty, the War on Drugs, and the War on Racism were all declared with fanfare, but they seem like intractable struggles, not unlike the Vietnam War. This has generated a pervasive sense of fatalism about these problems, a sense that there's nothing anyone can really do anyway—certainly not on an individual level. Somehow we got the impression that these were all global problems calling for global solutions generated by experts.

But every now and then this paralysis of analysis is shaken by actions taken from a different point of view. Consider an inner city high school where half of the students were expected to drop out before graduation. A national problem that points out the need for a comprehensive urban policy? Perhaps.

Volunteers in one school district didn't wait for an urban policy to come from Washington. Each volunteer focused on five students. The volunteers came to the school each day simply to extend a greeting to their five student friends.

"Hi, Bill, good to see you."

"Glad you're here, Leticia."

"Hey, Juan! How's it going?"

Remarkably, all the students in this simple experiment improved grades and behavior after only a few weeks. What they needed most of all was simple affirmation.

Public health officials in a mid-western city were deeply concerned that many pregnant women and mothers of young children with substantial health risks who were participating in a program to provide food and medical care were late for or missing their appointments. These regular checkups were a crucial part of a strategy to cut the infant mortality rate in this country, the highest rate of all the industrialized nations. A program called Love for Children recruited volunteers from area churches to call the women to remind them of their appointments and to provide transportation when needed. Within months, tardiness and absenteeism had dropped to half.

ARE WE GETTING USED TO FEELING
WITHOUT DOING?

There's one other factor that prevents people like Bill, the man I met on the airplane, from making even a modest contribution to people in need. Simply put, we're getting used to having strong feelings of compassion for the needy without taking any specific action. In recent years, network television has had many talk shows and news programs that specialize in human tragedy. These programs are designed to grab us, to elicit strong feelings of sympathy with the person in need.

Perhaps you saw the investigative television piece focusing on the children of fathers who refuse to pay child support after a divorce. The children were interviewed and we saw their pain. Along with a reporter, some of the kids tracked down delinquent dads and confronted them—all on camera. We saw fathers rejecting their own kids on TV. We saw the pain on the faces of their children.

Naturally, we get angry at those fathers and we wonder why the courts don't do a better job of enforcing child support payments. We feel terrible for the children as we imagine what it must be like. We feel intense sympathy for them. Then we move on to the commercial or switch channels to another program and the feelings dissipate. After all, how can we help someone who is only an image on a television screen?

I sometimes wonder if we are feeling brief moments of compassion more than ever before but doing less. If most of those feelings are evoked through the artificial means of television, we're less likely to act on them. We only have images in front of us, not people in need. For the sake of maintaining sanity we all learn to discount the feelings that television programs and commercials elicit. (Compare your response to the sight of a dead body on television or in person.) Is the media teaching us to ignore our feelings, getting us used to the idea that it is normal not to act when we feel compassion?

In contrast, Jesus of Nazareth, a man noted for his compassionate response to people in need, worked much differently.

The accounts of his life speak of him being "moved with compassion" when faced with human need. The word used in the original language of these accounts suggest a visceral response, a powerful feeling. But these strong feelings were always connected to specific actions as Jesus reached out to help those in need.

A CHILD'S PERSPECTIVE

I've noticed that children don't seem to be affected by these walls that keep us from viewing people in need as neighbors. They know little of sociological analysis and seem to suffer less paralysis. Their instinct when coming across a need is to act. A friend of mine was returning with his twelve-year-old daughter to the grocery store parking lot. They passed another shopper who was having problems with her car. As my friend got into his own car, he could feel the eyes of his daughter boring in on the side of his head. "Dad," she said, "I think that lady needs some help!"

Whenever I travel, I explain to my children why I must be away. One January it was a conference on helping the homeless which was sending me out on a snowy night. Four-year-old Laura called me back on my way out the door to add something to my suitcase. It was a piece of paper, pasted with cotton balls, that she had worked on diligently for an hour. "Daddy, will you give this blanket to a homeless family?" The "blanket" wouldn't keep anyone warm, but I was again touched by this childlike instinct to act.

A NEW PARADIGM

A paradigm is a way of looking at something that radically shapes how we perceive the world around us. A paradigm is a patterned way of thinking about things. In order to help people in need, we first need a new paradigm—a new way of thinking, a new way of perceiving people in need.

Charles Kraft, an anthropologist at Fuller Theological Seminary, uses the following diagrams to demonstrate what happens when we shift paradigms, that is, when we change our way of looking at something.[4]

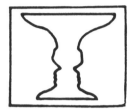

This illustration involves an easy shift. Depending on how your mind interprets the image, you see either a candlestick or, with a mental shift, the outline of two faces. Now try another one.

This is a more challenging paradigm shift. When most people first look at this illustration, they see an old hag with a large, unattractive nose. But if you look long and hard, your mind can shift its way of perceiving the same image and recognize a young woman with a long, flowing feather from her hat. (Hint: You're looking as if from behind the young woman and slightly to her left). I looked at this illustration for a full five minutes and finally had to ask my wife to trace the outline of the young woman. Perhaps you saw the young woman first and had to strain to see the old hag.

So we need a new paradigm—a new perspective on people in need. We need to see them as neighbors. Perhaps you remember the story of the good Samaritan told to a religious leader who asked Jesus, "Who is my neighbor?" The question was prompted by Jesus' assertion that the heart of religion is to love your neighbor as yourself. He then told a story about a man who was mugged by some roadside robbers and left for dead. Two different religious officials passed the victim and managed to view him as something other than a neighbor. Finally, a Samaritan, ironically a class of people despised by those who were listening to this story, came by. He did what was in his power to do to help the man: tended to his wounds and brought him to an inn, paying the innkeeper to look after him. In effect Jesus was saying, "That man in the road in obvious need is your neighbor. Think of him as your neighbor and treat him like you would a neighbor." The wounded man on the highway wasn't a client or a patient or the unfortunate but anonymous victim of crime. He was a neighbor.

Jane from Fairbanks, Alaska, tells of her experience helping a woman that she heard about through her church's ministry to needy individuals in the community. Jane experienced a paradigm shift.

When I was asked if I would drive Susan to a series of appointments, I was not happy. My impression of her was of a demanding and difficult person. I didn't want to get involved. However, I knew that God sees people differently than we do and I knew that He asks us to help the needy. So I decided to give it a try. That was the hardest part.

Once I started driving Susan and her two children, I discovered that she wasn't the difficult, demanding person that she seemed to be. She was just a mom with kids. I didn't have to act like a social worker. I could just be a friend. Each day that I drove, we talked. Out of that grew friendship. The last day I gave her a book of devotions and an encouraging note. She seemed surprised. She read the note and it really touched her. I saw tears come to her eyes and she gave me a hug. I can't believe how my attitude has changed.

Or consider another contemporary good Samaritan story. A mother and child were riding a bike along the road, when the child's foot was caught in the spokes of the wheel. A couple, Jenny and Rick, saw this happen in front of their home and went out to help. The child needed to be taken to the hospital for stitches so the couple drove them. When they took the mother and child home later that evening, they found that the family was living with their four children in a travel trailer.

The next day was a Sunday and Jenny and Rick were leading their adult Christian education class. They wrote up the incident in story form and asked the class what a person could do to help. After brainstorming, they came up with quite a few good ideas. Then they shared the good news to the class that this wasn't a story but a real family in need. Did the class want to put these ideas into practice?

The class decided to help this family find a home. An elderly woman in the class offered to loan them money at a low interest rate. Others provided help in securing a loan, finding a suitable home, and other details. The family moved into their new home a few months later. The class was able to relate to this needy family as neighbors.

The experience of this adult Sunday school class represents a growing trend. Individuals and congregations are beginning to realize they have a unique contribution to make to the massive social problems we face as a society. The welfare system is not the answer to human need. Ultimately, money is not the answer but people are—people who care for other people as neighbors, people who are able to see through the smokescreen of categories and statistics and reach out to help a needy person, one person at a time.

People like Carol, who was quite nervous the first time she delivered some groceries to a poor family as part of a church ministry to the poor. In the past, she had contributed money and food, but this was the first time she actually met any of those needing help.

When Carol arrived at the house, her tension evaporated at

the appreciation of the skinny little girl and her haggard-looking mother. Carol's eyes welled up with tears as the little girl hugged her. She seemed to be as hungry for affection as she was for food.

But then Carol saw the lice crawling all over the girl's head. She wanted to run, but something else would not let her go. "Oh Lord," she prayed, "This little girl needs my love right now... please hold me here so she can know your love." The Lord held her firm and Carol knew the thrill of becoming a partner with Jesus in revealing the love of the Father for the poor.

Carol wasn't trying to assuage middle-class guilt in the presence of the poor. Her arm was not being twisted to do some good deed. She was making a real connection with real people. She was seeing the poor with new eyes—as her neighbors. She had made the paradigm shift. And now she wanted to help. In fact, from that point on, you couldn't keep Carol away from people in need like that mother and her daughter.

In order to make meaningful contact like Carol made, in order to begin to relate to the poor as neighbors, most of us need some help. First of all, we will need to give some careful thought to where we can make the most effective contribution. And we will want to find some bridges to cross, bridges that connect our desire to help with a real person in need. As we consider various opportunities, we will face some important choices. Which ones should we say yes to and which should we decline? These are the challenges we will face in the next few chapters.

But the key to the kind of volunteering I am advocating in this book, the kind of volunteering that can make a real difference, is based on this fundamental shift in our perspective: behind every statistic cataloging social needs, there is a name and a face. We will only make a genuine impact when we begin to look beyond the need to see our neighbor.

FOUR

How Can I Help?

KIT AND DENISE, AN ATTRACTIVE, friendly and energetic young couple in our church, seem to be on everyone's list to recruit for various volunteer jobs. Unfortunately, they also find it very difficult to turn people down.

I noticed that Kit and Denise were not at church for several weeks. When I called to ask them how things were going, they confided that they were feeling overwhelmed—and a little irritated—by a string of requests for help. So they simply stayed away for a while to avoid the possibility of more requests.

I wonder how many people like this young couple—who have a sincere desire to help others—avoid the whole enterprise because they haven't learned how to focus their energies. They haven't assessed their strengths and limits and decided where they can serve and where they cannot. So when the request for help comes, they don't know how it fits into the bigger picture. They feel stingy saying no. Or how many people have felt burned by overextending themselves to the point where they are afraid to make themselves available at all anymore?

We are all limited human beings. We can't help every person in need who crosses our path. We can't volunteer for every needy cause. If you think that's what it takes to volunteer, you will give up before you even get into the game.

Even Jesus, a model of compassion and self-sacrifice, turned down some requests for help during his stay in northern Israel. On one occasion, he had spent a long evening helping the citizens of Capernaum. The next day, the people of that village urged him to stay with them. They needed more of what he had to give. But Jesus said no. He had other plans, other villages to go to. He knew that he had to focus his energies.

Volunteering is not an all-or-nothing enterprise. People who volunteer their time give an average of four hours per week. Some give less. Many give closer to ten hours a week. An extraordinary few give substantially more, usually because they have more time available than the average person.

Even those with a great deal of time and energy to give have to make choices: Where do I invest my resources? Whom do I help? What opportunities do I have to turn down?

Before you commit yourself as a volunteer to help others, consider a preliminary step. Spend a few weeks taking stock of what you have to give and where your time and energy would best be spent. I guarantee that you won't regret the time invested in this assessment, and it may save you a great deal of heartache down the road.

TAKE STOCK OF YOUR INTERESTS AND PASSIONS

Chances are you wouldn't be reading a book like this if you didn't have something inside tugging at you. You're not just interested in helping others because you know it's like eating oatmeal—"the right thing to do." You have yearnings, desires, promptings, inner inclinations to do certain kinds of things, or to help certain kinds of people. Pay attention to these urges. Don't discount them. If anything, give them plenty of oxygen and fuel and see if they don't fan into a flaming passion.

Dorothy always had a special place in her heart for new mothers. She had been a young, inexperienced mother herself and vividly remembered her feelings of insecurity and her desire for a more experienced mom to turn to. After her own children were out of diapers, Dorothy thought she was through with that phase of her life. At the same time, she wanted to share what she had learned with new moms who faced the same kinds of issues.

Eventually, Dorothy volunteered to help new moms through the La Leche League, an organization that provides coaching for mothers who want to breastfeed their babies. It was the perfect vehicle for Dorothy's concern. Volunteering to help these women was a joy, not an obligation. She didn't have to drum up the internal energy to help because the motivation was already there.

Of course you need to test your interests to see if they have what it takes to provide that kind of inner motivation that makes helping others a joy. It is possible to have a passing burst of sympathy for the problems of the inner city after watching a compelling movie. We can be made to feel a temporary concern or urge to help in many different areas. But which of these tap into a deeper well? What are the desires that keep coming back? You seem to bump into something that stimulates this concern wherever you go: a story in the newspaper, a TV news report, people you notice during your day, the account of a co-worker in touch with a particular need. These may provide clues to your deepest passions.

If you haven't given this area much thought, try filling in the blanks of the following questions, to see if they provide any food for thought:

1. I've always felt a special compassion for _____.
2. I seem to understand the problems of _____ better than most people do.
3. Whenever I hear or read about the problems of _____ _____ I am especially moved.
4. It bothers me that more is not being done for _____ _____.

5. When I think about helping others, I picture myself working with _____.

6. If I won the lottery and had to give the money to one group of people, I'd give it to _____.

7. If I were a teacher, I would want to teach _____
_____.

8. If I were a medical professional, I would want to help
_____.

The "Glad Gift" Inventory

A "Glad Gift" is something you can do pretty well and would enjoy sharing with others.

Name _____

Address _____

_____

Phone _____ Age _____

Available Hours: (Please check)

	Morning	Afternoon	Evening
Monday			
Tuesday			
Wednesday			
Thursday			
Friday			
Saturday			
Sunday			

Please check all categories of service you would be willing/able to provide.

___ Provide transportation to appointment in town

___ Help family move locally (have truck?_____)

___ Carpentry

___ Electrical Work

___ Plumbing

___ Yard work

TAKE STOCK OF YOUR LIFE EXPERIENCE AND SKILLS

Most of us tend to underplay many of the skills we've acquired over the years. It's a case of not seeing the forest for the trees. If you are skilled at something, it seems to just come naturally. It's easy for you to take it for granted, forgetting that it is a real skill. So don't pass quickly over this part of your personal inventory. Give it some serious thought and jot down some notes along the way.

___ Painting
___ Auto maintenance
___ Appliance repair
___ Home maintenance
___ Attorney/legal services
___ Physician or RN/ Medical services
___ Dentist/dental services
___ Counselor/counseling services
___ Teacher/educational services
___ Assist family in learning to reduce energy costs
___ Provide telephone reassurance for a single parent family
___ Be a special friend to a single parent mother and be a counselor to her
___ Mentor an at-risk child
___ Tutor an at-risk child
___ Tutor an adult
___ Budget planning

___ Provide sewing instruction for single parent mother
___ Establish a family friendship with an at-risk family
___ Form group from my church or other organization to develop/undertake a project on behalf of children
___ Share parenting skills
___ Share nutritional counseling/advice on grocery shopping, etc.
___ Translation help (Language: _____)
___ Financial aid (toward utility bills, rent, etc.)
___ Provide respite care for single mother or those with handicapped children
___ Other (Please specify)
_____
_____

Carol was a homemaker for several years when it came time to supplement the family income with part-time employment. Since Carol had married and started a family shortly after graduating from high school, she didn't have a lot of outside work experience. She wondered what she had to offer an employer. Did she have any skills beyond preparing meals, doing household chores, and driving the kids from one appointment to the next?

Volunteer Window of Work*

Directions: Please try to list 4 or 5 things in each pane of your Volunteer Window of Work. Your ideal volunteer position would tap into one or two Glad Gifts, reflect your preferences and avoid your No! categories.

Overarching Belief:
that caring volunteers
can change their communities for the better...
one life at a time.

Setting: the place/s you would prefer to work:
• at home
• in an office
• at a program site
• at the home of my client
• at a church/public place
• other?_____

Glad Gifts: any talents, skills, interests and hobbies that you do well and you would enjoy sharing:

_____
_____
_____
_____
_____

Note: Glad Gift suggestions are listed on pages 56 and 57.

Carol's husband, who had plenty of experience preparing resumés, sat down with her one evening and created a resumé. He pointed out his wife's organizational experience and expertise. Coordinating the schedules of six family members was in itself an achievement. Together they realized how many hospitality skills Carol had: overseeing the preparation of large dinners with several guests, caring for overnight visitors. She had

---

Relationships: With whom would you prefer to work?
• alone
• in a group
• with one helpee: __ a child __ a teen __ an adult

Quests: those thing you would like to learn more about or skills you might like to develop:

_____   _____

_____   _____

_____   _____

Time Available: or preferred work schedules:
• occasional service
• regular schedule: __ 1 x per week (1-3 hrs.)
                     __ 2 x per month (1-3 hrs.)
                     __ 1 x per month (1-3 hrs.)
• other _____

NO! please don't ask:

_____   _____

_____   _____

_____   _____

Volunteer Window of Work
Name of Volunteer _____

Address _____

* Window of Work prepared by Mary Jo Waters.

organized the Sunday school at her local church, helped younger moms informally, and coached a few friends at childbirth. When the evening was over, Carol was pretty impressed with her resumé.

I have trained hundreds of people to manage volunteers in local organizations. At first I was surprised to see how homemakers without much other work experience became such successful managers. These women taught me that a homemaker develops a wide range of management skills: scheduling, budgeting, planning, problem solving, mediation, confrontation, administration, time management, and many more.

In one community, seven homemakers were reluctantly involved in the training program for volunteer managers. Each felt she would enjoy the role but that she would not be able to do an adequate job with so little management experience. They secretly hoped I would confirm their suspicions by suggesting other roles. But I wouldn't. Five years later I learned that four of the seven women had started their own businesses. One had completed her high-school education and was enrolled in college. The seventh woman was still working as a volunteer despite a serious physical handicap. So now I am very suspicious when anyone tells me, "I'm not sure I have much to offer."

Your inventory of life experiences and skills should be more broadly based than an employment resumé. You probably have several skills you couldn't translate into a viable job but which could be invaluable for helping others.

For example, I enjoy athletics and have coached a few teams of younger kids. That doesn't make me a threat to Tommy LaSorda or Mike Ditka, but it might qualify me to help some kids keep out of trouble after school or during the summer months. It might provide a context for having a positive influence on some young men without dads. Perhaps you play piano—not well enough to go on tour but well enough to teach beginners at a youth center or a nursing home.

So consider the things you were involved in as a younger person including extracurricular activities from high school.

Consider your involvement in other organizations, churches, PTO, scouting. Think about hobbies or interests you have developed—current ones as well as those you haven't had time for in recent years.

Where did you grow up? Near a lake? If so, you may have boating and camping skills. Did you live in New York City so you know how to get around on a mass transit system? There are plenty of people who need to learn how to use a bus system. Do you know a foreign language? Did you help care for a mentally retarded brother or a grandmother with Alzheimer's disease? You may know a lot more about life than you think.

Do you know how to balance a checkbook? Do you understand that unless you pay your entire Visa bill each month you are going into debt at a high rate of interest? Do you know the ins and outs of grocery shopping—where to go for what, when to avoid the stores, how to make use of coupons? Have you had experience pushing a reluctant bureaucracy into action, for example, getting into closed courses at college or challenging a denial of payment on a health insurance claim?

All of these skills we easily take for granted may be invaluable to someone who has never had the opportunity or help to master them. More than that, they could provide the context for a relationship that says "Someone does care" to a lonely person lost in the shuffle of this complex world.

TAKE STOCK OF YOUR TEMPERAMENT

A basic awareness of your particular temperament—your style of relating to others, your outlook on life, your major personality traits—is an important element of your personal inventory. A sober awareness of what makes you tick will assist you in selecting a volunteer opportunity that will maximize your effectiveness.

If you have ever taken one of the vocational personality

inventories, dig out the results. The most commonly used tests are:

- Taylor Johnson Personality Inventory
- Meyers-Briggs Type Indicator
- DISC Inventory

Those who study the effective placement of volunteers indicate that understanding what motivates us is an important factor in selecting an effective volunteer role. Some people are primarily motivated by a concern for achievement. They have a strong desire for excellence. Such people spend a lot of time thinking about how to do a job better.

Others are more motivated by relationships. For these people, being with someone else and enjoying the comaraderie of a team effort are very important. They are more focused on the quality of relationships than on the particular task at hand.

Still others are motivated by a desire for influence. These people are more comfortable offering advice and more concerned for the impact they are having on others.

Each of these personality types has strengths and weaknesses, which can be taken into account in selecting a volunteer activity. For example, the person who is motivated by relationships will be more effective when he or she is working as part of a team or in a group context. The achievement-oriented person may be more frustrated in this setting if it doesn't support advancing particular goals. Someone who needs to have influence will be happier in a position of recognized leadership.

In considering your temperament, you will also want to take into account your current life circumstances. I have a friend who is gifted in working with the terminally ill. He is not intimidated by the emotional strain and relates well to people in that situation. But one year he lost his mother whom he had cared for in his home throughout a protracted battle with cancer. The same year he was involved with helping his next-door neighbor whose mother and father died within six months of each other—both of them at his neighbor's home. It was not the right year for my friend to volunteer time with the local hospice organization.

TAKE STOCK OF YOUR AVAILABILITY

If you're like me, your mind is spinning with good intentions—projects you plan to get to "someday." But unless you have a predictable time set aside for a given activity, it may become permanently stored in the "someday" file. You know that you really are serious about helping your neighbors in need when you sit down and ask yourself, "Now when am I going to do this anyway?" Defer that simple step and chances are you'll never get started.

If you've never blocked out a weekly schedule, including your work, sleep, and time for getting life's daily and weekly duties done, you might want to give it a try. This will greatly assist you in realistically assessing what you can and cannot do.

Determine, first of all, what kind of time you have available. If you are only available on an irregular basis because of job-related travel, unpredictable hours at work or other factors, it will limit what you can do—but it doesn't have to take you out of the game altogether.

Perhaps you can't find a regular weekly, bi-weekly, or monthly time, but you do have a week or two of vacation time available. Maybe an intense short-term investment is workable for you—a six week period twice a year where you can give some evening and weekend time. Or you may be able to find an evening or perhaps some weekend time each week or every other week.

Remember, 98 million Americans give an average of four to five hours each week in volunteer activity. Don't despair of carving out the time. Some employers provide for volunteer service during work hours. If your after-work hours are too limited, you may be able to select an activity that your workplace would gladly sponsor.

Volunteering can take place twenty-four hours a day, 365 days a year. Bill has an unpredictable work schedule, except that he is always free on major holidays. After spending Thanksgiving and Christmas alone, he decided to relieve the people who help out at the local shelter on those days when help is hard to find.

Even if you are free from one to five in the morning one day a week, you will be able to find something valuable to do.

Personal Schedule

Directions: Using the first scheduling grid, you may find it helpful to draw up a weekly, personal schedule. That'll help you determine the number of hours each week you really have available for volunteer opportunities. Using the second grid, then ask yourself the length of time you can commit to a particular volunteer activity. For instance, if you are a senior citizen with a fixed schedule, you may be able to commit a full year. But if you are a college student, you may only be able to commit time during a particular semester of study.

	Morning	Afternoon	Evening	After Midnight
Mon	_____	_____	_____	_____
Tues	_____	_____	_____	_____
Wed	_____	_____	_____	_____
Thurs	_____	_____	_____	_____
Fri	_____	_____	_____	_____
Sat	_____	_____	_____	_____
Sun	_____	_____	_____	_____

Service Commitment
___ 1 month
___ 1 semester (3-4 months)
___ 6 months
___ 9 months (school year)
___ 1 year

Many organizations formed to help people in need provide around-the-clock services. Shelters for the homeless typically need people from evening through early morning. Shelters for battered women have volunteers on call through the day and night. If grocery stores can attract shoppers around the clock, people are in need at all times of the day or night.

Some volunteer activities can be squeezed into small portions of time throughout the month. There may be a lonely widower who simply needs a brief phone call once or twice a week to say hello and see how he's doing. As you get to know him, you realize that you can easily lend him a hand without a big drain on your time. For example, you could purchase his few groceries when you do your own shopping or stop in on him on your way home from work once a month to help him pay some bills.

Part of the beauty of developing helping relationships one-on-one is the flexibility this can allow. Isolated people can be included in things you're already doing. The Meyers have five children under the age of seven. Loretta is busy at home and with church activities, and William is an architect by day and relief man at night for his wife. But this family has a wonderful way of including lonely people in their life—for Thanksgiving

	Sample Schedule			
	Morning	**Afternoon**	**Evening**	**After Midnight**
Mon	classes 9-12:00	work	exercise	
Tues	lab 9-1:00		work	
Wed	classes 9-12:00		class 7-9:00	
Thurs	lab 9-12:00	2–5 shop		
Fri	classes 9-12:00		exercise	
Sat		work		
Sun		exercise		

Winter Semester: January through April
2–5 every Thursday afternoon help Alice buy groceries.

dinner, a trip to feed the ducks at a nearby park, or some other family affair. They especially like to include people who love children and don't mind holding a baby.

TAKE STOCK OF THE OPPORTUNITIES
AT YOUR DOORSTEP

As you consider your desires to help certain people in particular ways and as you take stock of your skills, gifts, and availability, certain recurring pictures of what you might do will begin to emerge. These provide the pool of possibilities for you to seriously consider.

But as you begin to narrow the field of candidates, consider whether there are any opportunities staring you in the face. Sometimes God speaks to us from within, but sometimes he simply sends people to us or sees that our paths cross in a way that gains our attention.

Like many people, I was introduced to the joy of helping others by the quiet example of my parents. They never talked about voluntarism, but it was an essential part of their lifestyle. Visiting a sick person, making repairs on a disabled friend's home, sharing baked goods with a neighborhood family in need, spending time with a lonely widower—these expressions of love were as much a part of their lives as eating and breathing. As a child, I always knew were to find my mom if she wasn't home when I returned from school. She would be at someone's house like Mrs. Brown's or Aunt Sena's helping with a household chore, listening, or just being there.

A HIGHER PURPOSE

I believe that we have been designed by our Maker to have a focus in our concern for helping other people. "For we are God's workmanship," wrote St. Paul, "created in Christ Jesus to do good works, which God prepared in advance for us to do" (Eph 2:10). In some sense that I don't fully understand, arrangements have been made for the particular good works that I was created for. I can't do what you were designed to do, nor can you do what I was designed for. To me, that's part of the wonder and excitement of discovering what part we have to play in the bigger picture.

THE NEXT STEP

Once you have a focal point for your volunteer energies, one that takes advantage of your unique motivations and skills, it is time to consider what may be the most important step in translating your desire into a satisfying reality. It's time to start looking for a bridge connecting you with that neighbor in need.

FIVE

Finding a Bridge
to Someone
in Need

THE GOOD-HEARTED PEOPLE of a suburban church were determined to help the hungry people of a Los Angeles slum. They collected canned goods and other nonperishable food items and loaded them on a flat bed truck. The plan: park the truck in an impoverished neighborhood, surround it with volunteers, and distribute the food.

As they drove by convoy into the city, their first doubt about the operation's viability surfaced. The people about to receive these canned goods probably didn't have can openers, and there were none to give away.

Besides, this was looking like a pretty dangerous part of town. Was it really a safe place to set up shop? Maybe not. They made sure the truck doors were securely locked and tried to look inconspicuous. They looked for a friendly corner but found none.

Eventually, the urban missionaries came up with a new plan. "Plan B" is the topic of animated conversation in that neighborhood to this day. The volunteers climbed onto the back of the flatbed truck and tossed the cans of food toward the people on the sidewalks as the truck rolled along street. Yes, this really did happen. To say the least, it was not a satisfying experience for the helpers or the hungry.

A wealthy woman in California was moved to compassion by a television feature on homelessness in her city. She was determined to help. The woman called a local shelter with a well-intentioned, if misguided, pledge. "I want to contribute some money to help the homeless," she told the shelter director. "Can you tell me where I can buy some of those cardboard houses I saw on TV?" The shelter director didn't know how to respond. He appreciated her compassion but was discouraged by her lack of understanding. How could she not understand that the homeless people were so desperate for housing that they searched the city for cardboard boxes? What they needed was adequate housing and not more cardboard boxes!

I've had my share of misfires. Like my plan to help welfare recipients learn to manage their meager resources better. I persuaded several organizations in town to invite their chronically dependent clients to a seminar on "Managing Your Budget." Ever the salesman, I persuaded the agencies that this seminar would actually reduce their caseloads.

Alas, no one showed up. Looking back, I can laugh at myself. If you were on welfare would you feel a pressing need for better money management skills? Neither did anyone else.

I take some comfort in the gaffe of a literacy program coordinator who chose a busy shopping mall parking lot as the site of her advertising campaign. So she placed—yes, this really happened—flyers on the car windshields that read: "If you can't read this, we can help you! Call Julie at 761-4832."

When you get right down to it, many of us with the desire to help people in need haven't the first clue about how to go about it. We feel inept. And people in serious need may represent a whole different world that is unknown—and therefore frightening—to us.

THE UNDERSTANDING GAP

Take Al, for example—a "street person." Al exhibits some pretty odd behaviors. He walks with a wooden, shuffling gait. He drools constantly and his eyes seem to move around uncontrollably at times. He looks like a severely disturbed person.

Most of us would feel uneasy around someone like Al. What bizarre behavior will he exhibit next? Until you realize that these symptoms are all the side effects of some commonly prescribed medications for certain mental illnesses. The drugs control Al's psychiatric symptoms very effectively, but in a cruel twist, they create these strange physical manifestations. In fact, Al isn't as crazy as he looks. His mental illness is under control, but it's impossible for him to get a job with the side effects. Stop the medication, though, and the hallucinations come back.

Al's situation is not exceptional. There are people in every town who find themselves in the same bind. Like the lepers of old, they desperately need help, but their peculiar appearance frightens the people who might otherwise help them.

Most of us simply don't understand the problems of people in serious need. We're not to blame for the lack of understanding. It's just a fact. Consider, for example, Sara, who represents one of the common dilemmas of poverty.

THE ABC'S OF ADC

Sara is a single mother of three on Aid to Dependent Children. I invited Sara to meet with an adult Sunday school class at church. People in the class wanted to learn more about people in need.

We began by asking the group to work out a sample budget for Sara. Many people feel that people in Sara's position could find a way out by more responsible financial planning. So it was time to test that hypothesis. When the group looked over the facts about Sara's income and her basic expenses, they were incredulous. "Is this for real? There's no way we can produce a budget that works. There's just not enough money to go around." When I asked if anyone could suggest cost cutting measures for Sara and her family to trim out anything but absolute necessities, there were no volunteers.

Next question: Sara can get a service job at McDonald's for the minimum wage. Should she take the low paying job and get off the welfare rolls? The class agreed. This was the obvious first step. Until I explained that Sara would lose healthcare benefits and pay a large portion of her earnings for childcare. Should she still take the job? The class said no.

Final question: What do you think someone in Sara's position would most want from members of the church who wanted to help? The most popular answer from the class was "money." A way to buy herself out of chronic, mind-numbing need.

But Sara explained that she didn't want money. What she most needed was help caring for her children while she pursued job training. A total of eight hours of babysitting from two or three volunteers would enable her to take the classes that would prepare her for a decent job.

Sara's response was typical of mothers on welfare. When asked what needs to be done to improve the welfare system, they don't suggest more money, more food stamps, or any other commodity. They request what bureaucratic systems are least able to provide: a relationship with a caring person. Perhaps someone to provide a break from the kids, or even more likely, "someone to listen to me."

Welfare was keeping Sara and her family going. But welfare wasn't lifting her out of the cycle of poverty. She needed people—not just money—to help her move beyond dependence to self-reliance. And there were people in that church who were willing and able to help Sara. But they needed to understand her circumstances enough to know how to help in a way that made a real difference for Sara.

The key to helping people is indeed people. And I am convinced that people in our society want to reach out to the poor. But they are blocked. All kinds of dissimilarities keep them from making that critical connection: person to person. We live in a society of "haves" and "have-nots" who cross paths every day, but live in separate worlds.

WE'RE NOT ALL ICEBREAKERS

If you're reading a book like this, chances are that you are more than willing to help your neighbors in need. But because of the social and cultural isolation of people in need, you simply don't know how to make that connection. Many of us are like Bill, the man I met in the airplane who had a sincere desire to help the children of poverty in obvious need of adult influence. Bill saw their need through his car windshield, as he drove along the freeway. So what does Bill do to respond? Stop the car in one of those neighborhoods, get out, and announce to a group of pre-teens: "I'm here to help you become responsible adults! Where do we begin?"

Granted, some people have the personality and sheer nerve to dive right into helping others. They are like the icebreaking vessels used to keep the shipping lanes clear on the Great Lakes not far from my hometown. But icebreakers are specially equipped ships and most of us simply don't come with that kind of equipment.

BUT WE CAN CROSS A BRIDGE

If you are not built like an icebreaker, you need another way to make contact with people in need—someone who can be a bridge for you to cross. A bridge is a person, often within the context of a helping organization, who understands the people you want to help. A bridge-person knows where to find people in need and has already developed some credibility with these people.

In a sense, a bridge-person serves the purpose of the traditional Jewish matchmaker or yenta. The yenta made it her business to get to know all the eligible single women. Armed with that information she kept her eyes open for available bachelors. A good yenta was able to spot good matches and arrange for the two parties to connect.

The bridge-person is there to help you make the personal connection with someone in need—to match your resources with the needs of another human being. Without bridges we are reduced to throwing money at needs rather than lending a hand to a person in need. We are reduced to throwing canned goods at the poor as in the tragic comedy described earlier.

If you are interested in making the most of your time as a volunteer, the most important task you face is finding the right bridge-person to help you make contact with a person in need.

One of the most encouraging developments in the field of volunteering is the recent emergence of helping organizations and key staff people who serve in them in bridging the gap between people in need and people who can help.

LONG-DISTANCE BRIDGES

I was the speaker at a recent awards banquet in honor of hundreds of people who volunteered in the aftermath of the devastating earthquake that took place during the 1989 World Series in Oakland, California. I was introduced as a representative of World Vision, a Christian relief organization. Just then, a middle-aged African-American gentleman stepped into the aisle and walked deliberately toward the platform. As he approached me, he reached into the pocket of his suitcoat. He handed me a card and said with a great sense of dignity, "I sponsor a World Vision child." He flashed me one of the biggest and brightest smiles I've ever seen.

This man had been introduced to the joys of volunteering by participating in a sponsorship program offered by groups like World Vision and Compassion International. These organizations are a bridge for millions of Americans to children from impoverished countries around the world. Through the organization, a person of resource sponsors a needy child through a monthly contribution that provides educational, health, and other benefits for that child. The sponsor receives a photograph and a brief history of the child, and suddenly third world poverty has a name and a face. Sponsors are able to write to the child, pray for him or her, and, of course, contribute money that they know will make a difference.

Our family sponsors a child named Rachel from Zimbabwe. After four years, we feel a genuine connection with Rachel even though we haven't yet mastered her last name. You can see Rachel's picture on our refrigerator; and if you listen closely, you can hear my daughters praying for their friend, Rachel, most evenings. For our family, and for thousands of other people, this is a low risk introduction to the process of personalizing human need and taking a manageable first step to respond.

The sponsorship organization is a classic example of a bridge. The organization stands between the sponsor and the child. The organization takes great pains to connect the sponsor and the child. Giving money to a name and face is so much more satisfying, both to the person helping and the person helped, rather than the impersonal giving of money to faceless needs. Vast geographic distances make this the only reasonable strategy to connect those in our country who want to help with impoverished third world youth and their families.

Last year I found a way to apply the sponsorship idea in our own country. I visited five Catholic schools in the inner city of Detroit. Seldom had I been so by impressed the educational staff of any school. Despite inadequate budgets and blighted neighborhoods, these people were investing the leaven of life and love in their students.

I asked the principal at one of the schools if my young daughters could sponsor a student, whose parents could not afford the modest tuition, by sending in a monthly contribution. All I asked in return for the sponsorship fee was the first name of the student, a brief profile, and a periodic card or letter. It was arranged immediately and Emily and Laura are now the first sponsors in that school.

When I asked my daughters about sponsoring a child, they were thrilled with the idea. Immediately they personalized the need: Will we sponsor a boy or a girl? What is the student's name? Will we be able to meet our friend?

HOMETOWN BRIDGES

The distances that separate people in need from people with resources may be cultural and social rather than geographic. Bridges are needed to cross these gaps. But once a bridge is built, the payoffs are even higher because we have the opportunity to actually be involved face to face with people in need.

Let's look at several different hometown bridges. But before we do, remember, I am not trying to be an advocate for any one organization. I work for one of these organizations, World Vision, which sponsors LOVE INC, Project Hope Again, Love For Children, and other domestic programs. But there are many effective bridge groups around, including volunteer action centers at the local, state, and national level—a number of which are listed in the appendices. I want you, the person looking to make the most of his or her volunteer time, to be the customer for this book, not an organization. By describing the work of particular bridge organizations, I hope you will gain an eye for bridge organizations in your own town, so that you can find your way to the people you want to help. Some of the organizations mentioned here serve many different cities. They may be your next-door neighbors. Others are limited to a particular city. I mention these local groups because some of the most effective bridges in your hometown are probably homegrown, and they serve as examples of similar organizations that can be found "at a theater near you," if you look for them.

THE BANQUET OF SIOUX FALLS

The Banquet is the name of a ministry that provides free meals five days a week to some of the needy residents of Sioux Falls, South Dakota. Like many of the exciting new organizations to serve the poor, The Banquet is a cooperative effort of many different congregations. The volunteers who make The Banquet possible have learned how to set aside their differences and focus on their common ground in order to serve their community more effectively.

The Banquet is more than a name for the free meals program. It illustrates the philosophy behind the ministry. Listen to Carolyn Downs, director of The Banquet: "We are not a soup kitchen. In fact, our staff and board gear our efforts not to the poor people who benefit from the free meals but to the volunteers. We want to provide them with the opportunity to connect with the poor, our guests."

This perspective is the heart and soul of The Banquet. Their mission statement says, "We are here to build a bridge in the community between those who are disadvantaged, powerless, lonely and oppressed and those with position, influence, resources and strength." This is an organization that has a refreshing and powerful focus on people.

One of the volunteers who served in The Banquet moved to another city, where she promptly agreed to help out at the downtown soup kitchen. She was handing out silverware to those in line and greeting each person. Later, she asked one of the soup kitchen's veteran volunteers if she knew the name of an elderly lady holding a baby. "We don't talk to them," the volunteer replied. "You don't want to encourage them, do you?" The soup kitchen was providing a valuable service for the needy, but it was not serving as a bridge between people.

Those who serve at The Banquet would have a ready response to the statement, "We don't want to encourage them, do we?" Yes, we do want to encourage them! The Banquet is organized to provide a manageable opportunity for volunteers to meet, serve, and encourage their poor neighbors. In the process many of the volunteers find that the poor have much to give in return: a perspective on trouble, a word of thanks, the blessings that come with relationship.

Carolyn Downs describes the process of helping the volunteers help others: "Before each meal, we hold a half-hour orientation with each group of helpers to emphasize that we are not here for the guests but to be with the guests. A brief devotion is preceded by a question-and-answer time to diffuse any anxiety on the part of new volunteers. I usually assure the volunteers that interaction with our guests will come naturally; they just need to be themselves."

Carolyn continues, "Then after the meal, we spend time in a debriefing session to share what we've learned. Almost every night I hear someone describe how they had so much in common with the guests. Many are motivated to continue reaching out in Christ's name to help people they met at the meal. The biggest problem we have is finding enough opportunities for all the volunteers who want to participate."

If you're like me, you can't imagine yourself walking into a poor neighborhood with a truckload of groceries, looking for some needy people. But I'll bet you can picture yourself providing hospitality at a place like The Banquet. That's the difference a good bridge can make.

THE GENERAL STORE IN FRESNO

One of the words that describes the vision behind The Banquet is dignity. The poor were not treated like vagrants or bums. They were treated as guests. This is a key to bridging the gap between volunteers and those they help.

Cynder Baptista, a forty-five-year-old mother of five, wanted to help the poor by providing them with clothing. At first, she thought giving donated goods away was the answer. But then she discovered the importance of dignity to the people she wanted to help. They didn't just need clothes. They needed a little dignity. Or as Cynder told me, "They didn't need handouts. They needed a nice store with a place to try things on where they could pay reasonable prices and get some nice stuff."

The General Store was the fruit of this discovery. Formed in 1982, it has remained a sturdy bridge connecting members of Fresno's Northwest Baptist—a large, mainly white church—with the Latino and African-American families who live on the city's outskirts.

The store clerks are volunteers who get to know their customers. The relationships at the store provide the soil for new volunteer initiatives in the area. Shelly learned of the need for bilingual tutors after talking with some discouraged students. Bob started a youth group after noticing how some of the senior high students hung out at the store with nothing better to do. He didn't begin a ministry among strangers. These were people he got to know at the store. Other volunteers have led home visitations, Bible studies, delivery crews, and more.

The fruit of The General Store isn't measured simply in terms of people helped—well over 1,800—but also by the numbers of those who volunteer—a crew of 160. Christians volunteer at the store because it gives them the opportunity to help the poor without falling into the trap of mere check writing and donated throwaways. It's an opportunity to make a significant difference that doesn't require your whole life. And the store setting provides roles that are comfortable for the volunteer and supportive of the dignity of those who are helped. I know that I would feel a lot better about working as a store clerk, able to relate in a natural setting to people in need, than walking through a neighborhood handing out supplies. Again, that's the difference a bridge can make.

MOVING MOUNTAINS IN YPSILANTI

Cindy, the mother of three children under the age of two, was overwhelmed by her circumstance—and the laundry. After the birth of her third child, the laundry began to pile up.

Cindy didn't have enough money for the laundromat or the babysitting needed to tackle the mountain of dirty clothes. So the mountain grew for two full months. Seems like a pretty mundane problem, but imagine how debilitating it could be for that young family with so few resources.

Then Cindy heard about Wash With Care, a service provided by Hope Clinic—a free medical clinic supported by volunteers from several churches in the Ann Arbor-Ypsilanti, Michigan area. At the clinic laundromat, composed of six sets of industrial-strength washers and dryers donated by local congregations, Cindy met a volunteer named Joan who watched her three kids while Carol, another volunteer, helped Cindy with her laundry. They did twelve loads on Thursday, and finished with another ten loads the next week. Joan and Carol got to know Cindy in a natural setting. Their friendship became a real source of support to Cindy beyond the help with her laundry. To Cindy, it was a mountain-moving miracle of love.

Those who use the Wash With Care laundromat more than twice are asked to give some volunteer time in exchange. Cindy can bring her children and help staff the child-care room for others washing their clothes. Others snap fresh beans for a meal for the homeless, or help clean the Hope Clinic building. This breaks down that invisible wall between the helpers and the people being helped because the needy become helpers through programs like Wash With Care. The needy gain a sense of dignity as they interact with other volunteers as volunteers themselves. This is person-to-person volunteering at its best.

HOUSES FOR THE HOMELESS

Providing housing for the homeless is a task clearly beyond the reach of any individual. But Project Home Again has become a bridge between homeless families and churches who want to fulfill the biblical mandate to say more than "Be warmed and filled" to those without adequate housing.

Kathy was a young mother of two, who fled to a homeless shelter after repeated physical abuse from her husband. Becoming a single mom plunged the frightened young woman into poverty. But the shelter workers mentioned Kathy's plight to Joyce, the local Project Home Again director.

Joyce met with the homeless mother to see if she had the potential to become self-sufficient with the kind of help a group of church members could give. Convinced that Kathy could make it on her own with the right help, Joyce contacted a Methodist church which had expressed interest in participating in project Home Again.

Joyce met with six church volunteers to tell them about Kathy and her kids. The individuals agreed to work together as a team over the next year to help Kathy settle into adequate and affordable housing. They knew this would involve them in many different aspects of Kathy's life, but they also knew that it was a manageable task. No one person would need to be overwhelmed by the challenge.

After serving as a matchmaker, Joyce adopted the role of coach for these six church members who had never worked with the homeless before, but were willing to work together to make a difference for one homeless family. Everyone on the team had a role to play.

One team member worked with Kathy to search the newspaper ads for a two-bedroom apartment. Another talked with Kathy about managing her finances. Joyce was a resource person always ready to point out community services available to a person in Kathy's position. Another team member worked with Kathy to help find furnishings for an apartment. Someone else focused on helping Kathy secure a job, driving her around, arranging for babysitters during job hunting, even going shopping for clothes for Kathy to wear for job interviews.

Over time, Kathy discovered that she had six friends who were committed to helping her out of homelessness. The team let other church members know how they could pitch in since many in the church were able to lend a hand.

The church set aside fifteen hundred dollars to help Kathy get started. This covered a security deposit and first month's rent, some child care costs, and a few other items before Kathy got her first paycheck.

After a few months, Kathy was working in a job that paid her enough to get by, had moved into a two-bedroom apartment, furnished with the help of the church, and had arranged babysitting for her children. She was well on her way to financial independence with a little help from her friends.

Touched by the love she experienced, Kathy began to attend the Methodist church they all belonged to. It seemed she came to every conceivable event sponsored by the church. Eventually she became a full member. By this time, Kathy wasn't a homeless person on the outside looking in. She was a friend in need, climbing her way out of a dark hole.

The team of volunteers—aided by the Project Home Again coach—were able to help Kathy in a way that didn't foster dependence but gave her the boost she needed to make it on her own. The bridge organization helped the volunteers navigate the fine line between help that leads to real change and help that only becomes part of the problem.

Most of the families who are helped through Project Home Again can hardly believe it is true when they first learn that church members want to help.

The mother of a large migrant farm worker family who couldn't speak English sat dumbfounded when her family finished a planning meeting with the team of church volunteers. When the Project Home Again coach concluded the meeting by asking if anyone had anything else to say, tears formed in the mother's eyes. She slowly said something in Spanish while her ten-year-old daughter provided this translation: "My mother says there is nothing she can say, because there has never before been a day like this in our lives." This woman was learning to hope again, because people who were willing to help, but didn't know how, found a bridge to her family's need.

SOMEONE TO TALK TO

We often think of poverty strictly in material terms. But there are many people who suffer other forms of poverty. College students from faraway countries are a good example. For many of them, college is the first time they've been separated from their families.

I remember the time three men dressed in the drab garb of Communist China were wandering past my house, all focused on a large map as they walked. It didn't take a detective to realize they were lost. So I went out to see if I could point them in the right direction.

It turns out they were several miles from their destination with no public transportation nearby. I still don't know how they ever ended up in my neighborhood. So I drove them to the place they were looking for. In the car, I told them about an organization called International Students, a group that connects foreign students with American families and single people.

A host family with International Students has the student over for dinner on occasion and may even invite them to a holiday celebration. They may provide a weekly conversation partner to help the student practice his or her English. Older children, adequately supervised, make excellent conversation partners and usually enjoy reversing roles and showing an adult the ropes for a change. Families or individuals can give just a little of their time on a regular basis or become a more significant friend to the foreign student.

Some of the students, like most students, are financially strapped. But most of them are just lonely, isolated, and a bit disoriented. They don't need money or special counseling— just a friend, someone to talk to, someone to tell them how to use the city bus system.

The local staff person of International Students will probably know dozens of students who would love to get to know an American. He or she will be able to suggest cultural blunders to avoid and group activities to provide additional support. The staff person can introduce you to someone whose needs won't be overwhelming to you. In other words, the staff can be a bridge to connect you with the kind of person you are in a position to help.

LOVE INC

Dave and Joan were excited about their new arrival —a baby boy. But mixed with their elation was concern, because both Dave and Joan are blind. They knew they needed help to make sure that Johnny was well cared for.

The couple called LOVE INC, a network of Christians from several local churches who volunteer some of their time to help needy individuals and families. There are many Christians who want to do something to help, but they don't know how to reach the needy in their cities. That's where LOVE INC comes in. They screen requests for help to make sure they are legitimate and match the needs with the skills and interests of volunteers.

LOVE INC introduced Dave and Joan to Pam, a young volunteer from a nearby church. Pam knew a lot about babies and had two small children of her own. So Pam showed Dave and Joan how to feed, diaper, and handle their newborn son. They talked about preventing rashes and the best brand of babywipes. They talked about sharing responsibilities and finding enough sleep to keep everyone sane. Dave and Joan saw their son through Pam's eyes as she described Johnny's appearance to them in detail. But more important, they saw Jesus through Pam's friendship.

Dave and Joan didn't experience an organization meeting their needs. And Pam didn't experience helping as an agency volunteer. LOVE INC played the role that helping organizations are best suited to play—the bridge connecting people in need with people of resource.

LOOK FOR A BRIDGE

As more people are discovering the power of the person-to-person strategy for addressing the pressing needs of the homeless, the needy, the lonely, the elderly, and the children of poverty, we are seeing more bridges being built. Bridges like The Banquet, Wash With Care, Habitat for Humanity, LOVE INC, and thousands of others. As a person who wants to make the most of your volunteer time, I hope you can see the importance of finding a good bridge—one that will take your where you want to go, and one that will support you along the way.

SIX

Look before You Leap

S EVERAL YEARS AGO ON A FOGGY EVENING, a cargo ship ran into one of the supporting pylons of causeway near Tampa Bay. The highway above collapsed into the sea. Several cars traveling along the bridge in the low visibility of that dark night simply drove off the broken span, their drivers not realizing what had happened. One moment they were driving along a secure highway; the next, they were falling into the ocean.

Throughout the United States, there is a growing concern about the safety of the thousands of bridges within our network of roads and highways. Many of the structures are getting old, and too little money has been spent for replacement and repairs. These bridges are in need of inspection to see if they can support the traffic they bear each day.

In the previous chapter, we emphasized the need to find a bridge organization to help make a person-to-person connection with someone in need. But not all groups that work with volunteers are equally effective. Given the critical importance of this bridge organization, it is imperative that you carefully inspect the bridge before you cross it, because the condition of the bridge will have a great deal to do with the quality of your volunteer experience.

Twenty-five years ago, I served as a volunteer ambulance

attendant in a rural area. I had had no training, yet I was asked to tend to accident victims, stroke patients, and those suffering heart attacks. I lived in constant fear of either hurting someone further with my uninformed efforts to help or having an equally inept volunteer ambulance attendant help me after being injured in one of the high-speed ambulance runs.

I'll never forget the time we tried to transport a person who weighed at least three hundred pounds to the hospital. We helped her onto the narrow stretcher, then had to lift her to shoulder level in order to negotiate our way through a narrow doorway. We nearly dropped her!

Needless to say, the ambulance service was not a good bridge organization. They were stuffing any willing volunteer into a slot without much attempt to prepare the poor sucker for what he or she might encounter.

Fortunately, most organizations who work with volunteers are getting much better at helping volunteers succeed, but there are still plenty of rickety bridges. Consider, for example, the following ads for volunteer help.

Wanted: Volunteers desperately needed to handle crisis calls 24 hours a day. Emergency situation. No training or previous experience required. Call SOS-HELP Wednesday between 1-3 pm.

Wanted: Volunteers to assist a recent stroke victim in her home. Call 535-5555 persistently, ask for Ed.

Youth Volunteers Needed!
Every day in our county:
- 53 cases of child abuse are reported
- 12 children run away or are forced out of their homes
- 1,000 young people are living in out-of-home care
- 6 teens become pregnant
- A cocaine addicted baby is born, incurring two hundred thousand dollars in hospital costs

Maybe you can do something to help. Call Bill Henderson at 555-5555.

Yikes! Who would even stop to consider the crisis phone line position listed in the sidebar on page 88? Anyone who enjoys being thrown into emergency situations with no training and little back up. Most of us will turn the page and go straight to the comics. And for good reason. The sense of desperation communicated in these ads suggests that anyone foolish enough to volunteer will be thrown into a whirlpool of need that will suck him or her under within a few phone calls.

The stroke victim's family was still dealing with their own grief over their mother's disability. Their ad is an appeal for rescue with no real understanding of what kind of help is necessary or reasonable.

Without careful planning, training, and support, the volunteer who responds to a request could face a long list of unanticipated consequences. For instance:

- Without proper training in moving a paralyzed person, the volunteer drops the patient trying to transfer him or her from the bed to a wheelchair.
- Time demands multiply as family members are not able to abide by the schedule they first agreed to, falling back on the volunteer for "just a few more hours."
- The volunteer steps into the middle of long-standing family tensions as various members confide their concerns about others in the family to the volunteer.
- The relationship with the patient never gels because the volunteer is never given an understanding of how a person deals with the consequences of a stroke.

THE JOB DESCRIPTION FROM HELL

The administrator of a local hospital was reported to have the following expectations of volunteers. Anyone interested?

1. Hospital volunteers are expected to assist medical personnel on demand, no matter what the procedure, including invasive efforts, regardless of the patient's disease. Patients

who are HIV positive can be served by volunteers without the volunteers informed consent, if the staff determines that this involves a "reasonable risk."

2. All hospice patients (the terminally ill who are cared for at home) must have a volunteer assigned them even though some are as far as forty miles away.

3. When a home hospice patient dies, the volunteer is expected to go to the house, disconnect any intravenous lines or life support equipment, and prepare the body for delivery to the mortuary.

4. Hospital volunteers are expected to handle much of the paperwork for medical staff, including state forms and patient reports. Because they are not allowed in the nurses' station, they are asked to fill out the forms in a small volunteer office, without assistance.[1]

IT'S A BUYER'S MARKET

Don't get me wrong. There are thousands of wonderful volunteer opportunities available. But there are also plenty of disasters waiting to happen. So it is essential to abide by the well-worn dictum, "Let the buyer beware."

Keep in mind that it is a buyer's market for volunteers. Countless volunteer organizations are out to recruit you. *Grapevine: Volunteerism's Newsletter* reports that between 1987 and 1990, one hundred thousand new charities were created.[2] Existing organizations in the business of helping people are becoming even more dependent on volunteers as a changing economy forces smaller budgets for helping organizations in a time of increasing demands for services.

Did you know that volunteer administration is rated as a growth field? This specialty focuses on how to recruit, train, support, and encourage people like you. In other words, as a volunteer, you are very much in demand.

Yet I frequently hear volunteers express a low view of their value. "I'm just a volunteer," is a phrase I hope never to hear again. This attitude does little justice to yourself or the people you are helping.

As a potential volunteer, I want you to use your considerable status to influence the bridge organizations designed to help you help other people. By investing your time and energy in organizations that work most effectively with volunteers, you will provide a powerful incentive to all helping organizations to improve their services—to you and to the people you serve.

THE TEN-POINT INSPECTION PLAN

Before you volunteer your time helping others with the support of a bridge organization take some time to inspect the bridge, using the ten-point inspection plan.

1. Will this bridge connect me with a person in need? If an organization isn't able to bring you into meaningful contact with people in need, look for another bridge! Sadly, many organizations designed to help people are not able to connect volunteers with people in need. They may be more preoccupied with feeding the life of the organization than with assisting you to fulfill your resolve to help people.

I was once making a presentation to a foundation which provides funding for charitable causes—speaking on behalf of the children helped by a particular group. I was feeling a little pressure since the foundation's funding decision usually hinges on the presentation. Though I was tempted to support my plea for funds with an avalanche of charts and statistics, I found myself telling one story after another of people helped by the volunteers who crossed this particular bridge.

In the middle of my presentation, the foundation representative signaled me to stop talking. Usually not a good sign. So I was surprised when he said, "Thank you!"

"For what?" I asked.

"For talking about the children," he replied. He was used to hearing about goals and objectives, mission statements, strategies, and budgets, but not about people helped by other people.

So when you inspect a bridge organization, look for an answer to this question: Does the organization create helping relationships or does it merely manage tasks—or worse yet, simply give the appearance of addressing a need?

There is a church located in a run-down section of Detroit not far from the Ambassador Bridge, which links Detroit and Windsor, Ontario. It's a fitting location because this church is a bridge linking people with people. The church attracts participants from the suburbs as well as from the neighborhood, along with some of the homeless who are brought in from the Cass Corridor, the skid row of Detroit. The people of that church serve their neighbors in a thousand different ways—all person to person.

At one time the church belonged to an organization with an "urban mission" strategy, complete with well-articulated goals and objectives, an administrative staff, and a budget for serving the needs of the inner city. But the administrative apparatus didn't do much to connect people with people. At times I wonder if it spent most of its resources in studying the needs of the inner city, attending colloquiums on the needs of the inner city, and discussing mission strategies for the inner city, rather than helping people make a personal connection with the residents of the inner city. Now, that local congregation involved with the people of that neighborhood would be an effective bridge. On the other hand, the organization with an urban mission strategy had all the trimmings but less of the beef.

An effective bridge organization will have more than a clear sense of mission, goals, and good accounting procedures, necessary as these are. But the people who make up the organization will be driven by a singular passion: to help people like you develop a meaningful connection with people in need.

The people who are part of effective bridge organizations

speak of people as people—not units served, or needs met, or bits of statistical data. They have a sense of excitement about people; they love to tell stories of the woman and her two kids who were helped last week by a young volunteer couple. They have fresh stories to tell rather than simply repeating the legend of the person helped long ago in dramatic fashion.

2. Will the bridge organization give me an opportunity to make a difference? When we asked those familiar with volunteer opportunities to list selection criteria for those seeking to give their time and energy, we heard a similar refrain:

- "Is there an exciting vision, one worth pursuing?"
- "Does my contribution as a volunteer make a difference in the success or failure of the cause?"
- "Does this organization have work for me to do or are they just looking for warm bodies?"

Study after study on the factors that contribute to a successful volunteer experience rank "making a difference" among the top reasons people volunteer and stick with it. People who know they are having an impact for good in another person's life will overcome many obstacles to keep doing what they are doing. They don't want to get out of serving. You can't keep them from serving. Volunteers report losing interest in what they are doing when they have little sense of impact.

The volunteer mentors of four hundred high risk high-school students surveyed from locations throughout the nation learned that 87 percent of the students either enrolled in college or planned to attend college within a year of high school graduation. Nearly three-quarters of the students said that their mentor helped them raise their goals and expectations. So it's not surprising that 92 percent of the volunteers reported enjoying the experience and 86 percent said they were ready to be a mentor to another at-risk student. These volunteers knew they were making a difference.

When it comes to helping people, it's not always easy to know whether or not you are really making a difference. How many parents expend untold energy on raising their children, yet wonder, "Is anyone listening?" Human needs are not often responsive to quick fixes. It's not always easy to measure something as elusive as impact. It's easy to tell whether a high-school student has been helped toward the goal of graduation or attending college. It's much more difficult to measure the difference it makes to befriend the resident of a nursing home who has no other visitors.

But we know from our own experience that a caring individual who is simply there for us in a time of need is invaluable. Think about that friend who called you regularly after your mother died, just to see how you were doing. Or the neighbor who stopped by with a meal once a week when you were laid up with a bad back for three months. We had some friends who did just that a few years ago when my wife suffered a serious knee injury—and we won't forget their kindness. Did it speed her recovery? Hard to say. Did it make a difference? We're certain it did.

3. Does the bridge organization have plenty of satisfied customers? A good bridge organization will view the volunteers who work under their umbrella as their customers. They are wired to see that these people are well served in their serving. So before you commit any substantial time and energy to working with a particular bridge group, talk to a few customers.

The best recruiters for a good college football program are not always the coaches but other players. The players will give you the inside scoop: how practices are run, how players are treated, how football is balanced with studies, what life on the campus is like. The best recruiters for volunteers are not the paid volunteer recruiters but other volunteers.

Each bridge organization will have its strengths and weaknesses. Some projects will be more effective than others. Some people will be better to work for than others. Other volunteers will provide you with invaluable information.

Above all, find out whether the volunteers who have crossed a particular bridge have that experience of making a meaningful difference. Do they radiate a sense of satisfaction, even in the face of challenges? Or do they seem frustrated? Do they seem to feel overwhelmed by the task? Or do they have a reasonable role to play?

Do they love what they are doing, for all its challenges and frustrations? The women who serve in the Missionaries of Charity, a group founded by Mother Teresa to serve the poorest of the poor, love what they are doing. The organization behind the ministry sees to it that the people who serve are well suited for the rigors of that particular mission. If there is an effective bridge supporting even the people engaged in the most challenging tasks, those involved will love to do what they are doing—in spite of all the frustrations that come with the territory. They will be satisfied customers.

4. Is there a person in the bridge organization who is looking out for you? A good bridge is well connected on both sides of the river. A good support organization for your volunteer time has to be well connected to the people you want to help and well connected to you. If the bridge is only well connected to the people you want to serve, but doesn't take an active interest in helping you be effective in your role, chances are good that you will feel like you are being thrown to the lions—thrust into the jaws of overwhelming need with little sense of how to respond.

Bridge organizations who are well connected to your side of the river will often have someone called a volunteer coordinator. It will be this person's job to assist you in your goal of making a meaningful connection with someone in need.

The members of the church who helped the young homeless mother move into her own apartment through Project Home Again, a bridge organization described in the previous chapter, were coached by a Project Home Again staff person named Joyce. Joyce was the person who told them about the program, who helped them decide if they could participate, and who was available with important information and support along the way. Joyce wanted the homeless family to be helped and she wanted the volunteers to have a meaningful and manageable experience so that others would be encouraged to help in the future.

A good bridge organization may not have a full-time person who is called a volunteer coordinator, but there will be someone in the organization who has your interests as a volunteer in mind. It may be the leader of a church-sponsored ministry, or an experienced volunteer who is concerned to help other volunteers have as good an experience as he or she has had. Whoever it may be, there will be somebody.

Before volunteering, have a good talk with that person. Does he or she seem to be competent, concerned for the people you want to help, and concerned to help you? If you don't come away from that discussion with a sense of confidence in the volunteer coordinator (or equivalent) you may want to look for another bridge to cross. And if you can't find that person on the bridge who seems to be looking out for you, you should think twice—even three times—before crossing.

5. Is training available to help you make a difference for someone in need? Even the early Christians who were thrown to the lions in the colosseum were given a few tips on how to last long enough to put on a good show. So it's not asking too much to seek some coaching in the initial phases of your volunteering.

Naturally, your need for training will vary with your own experience, abilities, and the volunteer opportunity you are considering. If you're helping to serve a meal that's already prepared in a local soup kitchen, you'll probably only need a brief orientation and a more experienced volunteer to work with at first. If you are helping to prepare the food, you will need training in health and safety concerns. Dishes should be washed with hot water at a certain temperature; certain foods shouldn't be left at room temperature for long; and so on. If you're running the kitchen, you'll need considerably more training.

Good training should provide you with information about any legal issues that you need to be aware of as a volunteer. What can you do to avoid running into legal potholes during your volunteering? What steps can you take to protect yourself from legal liability? For example, many organizations recommend that their volunteers not spend time alone with children they are serving as a protection against charges of abuse. Certainly a male volunteer should not spend time alone with a woman in her home. Simple preventive steps like these are often the best protection in our litigious society. Look for them in a good training program.

I am convinced that many of us don't offer to help more, not for lack of concern, but for fear of botching the job. Take teaching someone to read for example. I'm a good reader myself and I've helped my own children learn to read, but teaching another adult to read seems like it might be a different undertaking. If I were to volunteer as a mentor to teach someone to read, I would sure appreciate a little help on how to go about that particular task.

Effective training moves us from a position of fear and insecurity to a place of confidence. My mother always dreamed of being a teacher but never had the opportunity until she became a volunteer late in life. She was hesitant at first about her ability to tutor two Hispanic boys, but she received excellent training. Those boys were helped and my mother's dream was realized.

6. Is there a clear job description? The absence of a written job description for a volunteer position may indicate that the organizers haven't taken the time to think through what the job requires. Other key elements for supporting volunteers may be missing as well.

As a volunteer, you can add critical support to people in need. You can lend a hand. But you are not the solution to the person's every problem. You are not a savior. Without a clear understanding of how you can help, you may easily feel overwhelmed by the needs you encounter. You may try to meet needs that you are in no position to meet. Or you may simply shrink back as you sense the powerful pull of what seems to be a black hole of need from which there is no escape.

A well-considered job description provides the boundaries you need to be an effective volunteer. If you are available to support a single mom with young children, are you expected to provide parenting assistance in the form of advice, or are you expected to provide babysitting whenever the need arises? How much time are you expected to give? And what kind of support is within your available resource to provide? Does the young mother need someone to talk to about caring for young children, or is she seriously depressed and in need of professional care? A job description provides the answers.

A good job description should answer the following questions:

- Whom am I helping?
- What time commitment is expected?
- What kind of time is involved (evenings, daytimes, weekends, regularly scheduled, or "as needed")?
- What kinds of needs should I take concern for?
- Are there any obvious needs that I should not become involved with because of my own lack of qualifications or the person's particular circumstances?
- Over what time frame should I expect to provide this support (one time, six months, a year, indefinitely)?

It is not essential that all of these questions be answered in a written job description for every conceivable volunteer opportunity. The good Samaritan didn't have a written job description before lending a hand to the injured traveller. But for volunteer roles arranged through a bridge organization, you are wise to find answers to these kinds of questions before you jump into a helping role—for your sake as well as the sake of the person you will be serving. Talking these issues over beforehand allows you to take an active part in shaping the definition of your role as a volunteer.

Sample Tutor Job Description

Evaluate this job description using the criteria I've just mentioned.

Adult Basic Education Program

Hours:_____ Location: _____

Supervisor: _____

Beginning date:_____ Ending date:_____

Skills required:

1. High school diploma or equivalent.
2. Patience to let student progress at own pace.
3. Ability to analyze student's strength and weakness.
4. Flexibility to adapt to student's acceptance of activity.
5. Creativity to eliminate repetition and boredom.

Training required:

1. Attend 30-minute orientation and observe tutor working with student.
2. Attend planning session with teacher prior to beginning assignment.

Goals and Objectives:

1. Know student and student goals.
2. Provide student with positive feedback.
3. Make sure student accomplishes some task, whether large or small, before he/she leaves session.
4. Establish rapport with student to maintain a close relationship.

Job Description:

1. Tutor works on a one-on-one basis with student to help student learn and accomplish his goals.
2. Tutor works under direction of teacher even though sessions may be held in locations other than classroom.
3. Tutor assists student in charting goals and keeping record of achievement.
4. Tutor tries to help student take responsibility for his or her own learning.[3]

7. Is support available once you begin to help? My brother, Mert, signed up for a program that links volunteers with prisoners who could benefit from a relationship with a friend from outside. The training Mert received was helpful and he felt prepared to develop a relationship with a prisoner. The program director assigned him to a prisoner named Ray.

Mert's first visit with Ray was not what he had expected. Ray was criminally insane. His attention span was very brief; his thoughts, disjointed; and it was virtually impossible for him to relate to my brother.

Mert visited Ray several times. But there was no sense of connection at all. Each visit found Ray in a different world. Reluctantly, Mert asked the program director for a new assignment. "I really want to form a relationship with a prisoner," he emphasized.

The program director sympathized with Mert but refused to give him a new assignment, saying, "Ray has been on the list for so long." My brother has not given up on Ray, visiting him regularly for several years. But Ray is still beyond the reach of a nonprofessional, and Mert is filling a slot. The program director hasn't been able to provide any meaningful support to Mert for working effectively with someone like Ray. This is not the kind of volunteer experience I would wish on any reader.

When you are helping someone in need, you may run into situations that you don't know how to handle. The person you are mentoring may need help affording to keep his or her heat on in the winter, or the person may be short on groceries. To whom do you turn for help when that happens? Is there a person on the bridge who can lend you a hand when you find yourself unsure about what to do? This person, often the volunteer coordinator or the leader of a particular program, may not be able to answer all of your questions, but he or she will be able to put you in touch with someone who can help. Perhaps it will be another experienced volunteer who has faced similar challenges or a professional in a particular field. Good bridge organizations are committed to providing this kind of backup to volunteers.

8. Does the bridge have a reputation for integrity? As in any human endeavor, organizations which specialize in helping people can attract con artists who appeal to your compassion for people in need in order to provide for themselves. So before you serve under the umbrella of a particular bridge organization, make sure you are dealing with the genuine article. "When in doubt, check 'em out." These are some things to look for:

- Is there an annual report available, with an accounting of all income and expenses?
- Is there a governing board with people of integrity on it?
- Does the organization have a good reputation in town with people who have interacted with it?
- Does the organization enjoy the support of other organizations you trust?

If you have any doubt about a particular group, seek out some good character references for the organization's integrity. The following people are often in a position to provide helpful perspective:

- The pastor of your local church
- The Salvation Army in your town
- Other reputable charitable organizations
- Friends in the helping professions (social workers, doctors, teachers, etc.)
- Volunteers who have served with the organization in question

9. Does the bridge organization rely on guilt, desperation, or pressure tactics to recruit you? You can learn a great deal about a bridge organization by the way it approaches you as a prospective volunteer. Does the organization have a positive vision for you as a volunteer, or do they rely on an appeal to guilt as a primary motivator? Organizations that rely on guilt-inducing appeals for help often do so because they lack a positive vision and are not effective in attracting and supporting volunteers.

If you sense desperation in shrill appeals for volunteer help, you may also have a reason to look before you leap. Sometimes the desperation is justified by the circumstances (for example, urgent appeals which stress the nature of a devastating natural disaster). But sometimes a desperate appeal is a sign that a bridge is not doing its job well. That is, volunteers are not choosing to use it because it isn't in good shape. If a real bridge were in disrepair because it wasn't generating enough income in tolls, would you respond favorably to an appeal to cross it?

Pressure tactics in recruiting are another bad sign. If you need a few days to think over a request for help and find yourself being pressed to give a quick answer, give a quick no instead.

10. Does the bridge organization value volunteers enough to say thank you? By now, you've probably gotten the message that a good volunteer organization should be friendly toward volunteers! That means saying "thanks!" in different ways. This attitude of gratitude may show up in a volunteer newsletter. It may be evident in the person serving as a volunteer coordinator. The organization may sponsor an annual volunteer appreciation banquet. There are many different ways to express appreciation.

The expression of this gratitude for your volunteering is an indication of a well-built and well-maintained bridge. It may not be critical as an isolated characteristic, but it says a great deal about whether an organization values its volunteers or takes them for granted. If you have the choice, give your time to the organization that values your time.

HOW CAN WE HELP YOU HELP OTHERS?

Just as companies have a corporate culture driven by a set of values that express themselves in the way the company does business, helping organizations have their own culture determined by their values. After several years of working with many different helping organizations, I've observed that the most effective ones are those which place a high value on supporting their volunteers in the critical task of assisting people in need through building a helping relationship.

This core value—"How can we help you help others?"—has a way of working its way through the whole organization. It's one of the first things you notice about the way the organization does business. These are the organizations and programs that can become a solid bridge connecting you with that neighbor in need. When you find a bridge that passes inspection, you're in business.

SEVEN

Yes or No?

"HOW DID I GET INTO THIS?" Jim asked himself as he approached the two-bedroom ranch style home. He had agreed to go door to door raising funds for the March of Dimes, but his heart wasn't in it. Why did he feel this way?

Jim always contributed to the March of Dimes and he supported the concept of giving for medical research. But as he thought about his lack of enthusiasm for the task at hand, he realized that he had never really said a clear yes to this volunteer opportunity. It's just that he never said no, and now he was part of the campaign. He didn't want to disappoint the friend who had recruited him.

We all tend to give a greater effort to activities that we have enthusiastically agreed to. This is especially true of volunteer service, which normally comes from our discretionary time. Knowing how and when to say yes—and no—to a given opportunity to help others is an important aspect of serving wholeheartedly.

WEAK REASONS TO SAY YES

A weak yes provides a weak foundation for volunteering; it is easily questioned once challenges arise. A strong yes provides a much firmer foundation. The difference between the two is often a matter of motivation: A weak yes is fueled by weak motives; a strong yes is fueled by strong motives.

"I felt guilty saying no." Perhaps you've run into those young people selling various products door-to-door who present themselves as disadvantaged youth seeking to better themselves. Before offering to provide you with a five-gallon container of concentrated cleaning solution, they make sure you understand just how disadvantaged they are. Rather than persuade you about the superiority of their product, they appeal to your sense of guilt. If you do turn them down, they have a thousand and one ways of making you feel guilty.

Feelings of guilt are well designed to gain our attention when we've done something wrong, but they are very weak motivators. If we say yes to a particular request simply to avoid feeling guilty, we are likely to feel resentful later on—as if someone were forcing us to do something against our will. Our yes didn't come from the heart; it came from a desire to avoid an unpleasant feeling.

"I didn't want to upset the person asking me." The other day, someone who claimed to be from a Police Officer's Association called to solicit a donation. I prefer not to commit money over the phone to an organization I am not familiar with, so I gave my customary speech to that effect. The person soliciting funds—I wonder whether he was a police officer or a professional fund raiser—began to apply various pressure techniques. As he was making his pitch, the following thought occurred to me: "I wonder if this is a policeman. I'd hate to have a policeman upset with me!" I imagined myself pulled over for a speeding ticket with a burly police officer glaring down at me saying, "So you're the guy who wouldn't contribute a lousy ten bucks to the Police Officer's Association!"

Since I've been on the other end of raising funds more than few times, I understand people will do almost anything to appease the fundraiser. One type of donor habitually pledges to give to everyone who asks, but he rarely follows through. His pledge is just an easy way to get the fundraiser off his back.

Most of us have an instinctive aversion to conflict. More than anything, we want to avoid rocking the boat. So if someone presents an emotional appeal for our help, we begin to imagine how upset they will be if we don't agree to the request. Our yes, in that case, isn't a yes from the heart. It's a concession to fear. Fear is effective in preventing us from taking certain actions; but as a motivator for positive action, it is weak.

"I didn't want to look selfish." Perhaps it's happened to you. You are sitting in a group with ten others. Someone presents a pressing need: after a painful divorce, they need help moving from a nice home into an apartment. You would love to help, but your mother is seriously ill and needs all the attention you can give her. But the person in need asks for an answer from everyone on the spot. One by one everyone agrees to help. At last, all eyes are on you. You can barely believe your ears as your own voice betrays you. "Sure, I'd be glad to help." Anything else would have sounded incredibly selfish.

A week later you show up to help at the agreed upon time in spite of your hectic schedule and with misgivings about your priorities. Only half of the original volunteers are there. Everyone else has called to say they can't make it for one reason or another. You put in your time, wondering what you're doing there—and kicking yourself for saying yes when you really meant no.

THE POWER OF A YES FREELY GIVEN

A fundraiser for famine relief twenty centuries ago gave some good advice to those who received his appeal: "Each man should give what he has decided in his heart to give, not reluctantly or under compulsion, for God loves a cheerful giver" (St. Paul, 2 Cor 9:7).

In so many aspects of our lives—from paying taxes to cutting the lawn, and at times, dragging ourselves to work—we sense at least some measure of compulsion. To some extent, we do these things because we have to. But volunteering is an opportunity to give freely. It is important that we learn the power of a yes freely given.

I worked for several years at a crisis clinic. The place lived up to its name because we helped people in all manner of trouble. One lady called because her husband was shooting his gun off in the house. We called the police. A family called after being evicted from their apartment. A college student called who was contemplating suicide. The clinic found that in many cases, volunteers—trained by the staff but not experts in the field of crisis intervention—were just as effective as a psychologist or social worker. The volunteers always seemed to bring a genuine sense of enthusiasm to their work. It was obvious that they liked to do what they were doing. The volunteers weren't just doing a job. They were people helping people and loving every minute of it. More than the paid staff, the volunteers were operating under the power of their yes, freely given.

HOW TO SAY NO WHEN THE NEED ARISES

Margaret's sister loved her volunteer work at a church sponsored retirement home. She had a wonderful time with several of the elderly residents. She would feed them every day—and get them to smile. When her volunteer partner moved to Florida, Margaret's sister tried to recruit her services as a new partner. As a recruiter, her sister was very compelling.

When Margaret first heard about the opportunity, it seemed appealing. But as she prayed about it, she was surprised at the absence of any confirming sense at all. Margaret had learned to listen to that "still small voice," so she reluctantly told her enthusiastic sister no.

"I spent a few weeks feeling kind of guilty," Margaret reports. "But then I received a call from my pastor asking if I could serve on a team to help resettle our church's new Vietnamese immigrant family. I leaped at the chance with a whole-hearted yes. My son is married to a Vietnamese woman, so I was eager to help and learn more about her culture. And I no longer felt guilty about the retirement home. I am convinced God was saving me for something else."

If you are the kind of person who finds it difficult to say no, here are some options to consider when you sincerely believe that a no is required.

1. Ask for time to consider the request. Sometimes in the face of a high-powered presentation, you may simply feel uneasy about saying yes without having a well-considered reason. That's a good time to say, "I'd like to give serious thought to this possibility. Can I call you back in a few days?"

Then, away from the pressure of an expectant recruiter, you can consider the opportunity. This may lead to a stronger yes—one that is freely given—or a thoughtful no.

2. Say no, with explanation. If you have a good reason for turning down a request for volunteer help, let it be known. It is often a help to the person asking and communicates to them that you've taken their request seriously. If you are declining an opportunity to volunteer because the bridge organization didn't pass inspection, do the organization (and those they serve) a favor: tell them why. Your honest observation may provide the insight and motivation needed for the organization to change. They may be able to respond to your concern and open a door to an effective volunteer opportunity for you or for someone else.

3. If you feel unduly pressured, just say no nicely and repeatedly if needed. When I think I'm being worked over by someone seeking my volunteer time—and I'm sure that this is not an opportunity for me—I will select a simple phrase and when pressed, simply repeat it. In assertiveness training courses, this is called the broken record technique. Here's an example:

"So do you think you can help us out with this, Ms. Ellison?"

"No, I'm afraid I won't be able to."

"Gee, the need is really great, Ms. Ellison. We sure wish you could help."

"I understand, *but I'm afraid I won't be able to.*"

"Why not, Ms. Ellison? We all need to do our part."

"Yes, we do, *but I'm afraid I won't be able to.* But thanks for asking."

4. Say no to the specific request, but offer what you can do instead. If a request for help is beyond your resources, offer what you are willing to do as an alternative. "I don't think I could visit Mrs. Rothstein every week, but if you find someone else, I would be glad to substitute for them when they can't make it."

5. Offer ideas or suggestions for finding someone else. If you've ever done any recruiting for volunteers, you know that having a list of interested people is invaluable. So if you are not able to respond to a worthwhile need, consider whether you could suggest other possibilities for the person seeking a volunteer. You might offer to post the request on a church bulletin board or at the office. Or you might offer to mention it to a friend you think may be interested. As a courtesy, don't give out a friend's name unless you have your friend's permission first.

HOW TO SAY YES

Here's some things to keep in mind when you are ready to accept an opportunity to volunteer.

1. Don't say "I do" until you know that you can. Jesus said "Let your yes be yes, and your no be no." If we agree to help out, we should be in a position to follow through. That calls for some thoughtful consideration, *before* saying yes. This is a service not only to yourself but also to those who are counting on your help.

I've learned—the hard way—to restrain myself from impulsively saying yes without counting the cost. Rather than give an immediate "Yes, that sounds great!" I'll express optimistic interest. "Offhand, that sounds promising.... Tell me more about what's involved."

While you can freely express interest, be careful not to say "Yes, you can count on me" until you are prepared to make good on your word.

2. If your yes is conditional, make the conditions clear. It's easy to say "Yes," when you really mean, "Yes, as long as...." Before you say yes to a volunteer opportunity, consider whether there are any non-negotiables to spell out. Are there out of pocket expenses you can't afford to cover? Do you have any safety concerns that must be met? Are there support services that you can't do without? You'll spare everyone a great deal of trouble if you make these conditions clear at the time you agree to help.

3. Be specific about what you are agreeing to. It is almost always a good practice to state your understanding of what you are agreeing to as part of the process of saying yes. A written job description serves this purpose very well, but at the very least, restate your understanding of what the responsibility of a specific job entails. "As I understand it, this is what you're looking for. Is that correct? Yes? Well, I'd love to do that."

4. If you are unsure about how it will work out, consider agreeing to a trial period. Volunteering often brings us into the realm of new adventures. We're trying out new skills or venturing into uncharted territory. Like the time I volunteered to coach my daughter's soccer team. Actually, my wife Kathy volunteered me. I didn't know much about soccer and less about coaching. Since I was coaching with another father, I knew I had a way out if worse came to worse. When my co-coach asked the girls at the first practice to raise their hands if they were afraid, I'm afraid I was the first to raise my hand. But I was willing to give it a try.

When you are engaging in something new, one of your smartest moves is to suggest that you field-test your interest by serving as a volunteer for a few weeks before making a final decision. This gives you the freedom to try something that stretches you, without feeling that you will be locked into an unworkable situation. The knowledge that there is a way out of an unworkable situation allows you to relax and increases your chances of success.

The point of all this advice is not to insure that you protect yourself against every potential problem. To be satisfying, volunteering will call for real sacrifice. But I want it to be meaningful sacrifice. I want you to be wholeheartedly engaged in helping where you can make the most impact, that is, focused on making a real difference in the life of someone in need. To do that with enthusiasm and conviction is good for you and even better for the person you are helping.

EIGHT

A Time to Give

LIKE THE SEASONS OF THE YEAR, our lives flow from one season to another. Childhood gives way to the twenties, thirties, midlife, and the golden years. Each season brings its own set of challenges and opportunities. College students seem to survive the late nights of dorm life without much difficulty. Try that in your forties and you have an instant appreciation of the wisdom of the ages: "There is a time for everything, and a season for every activity under heaven."

SEASONALLY ADJUSTED VOLUNTEERS

If I were to ask which season of life was most suited to volunteering, you would probably picture a retired homemaker volunteering her time at a local hospital. In fact, seniors do have unique contributions to make in helping others through volunteer efforts in many different areas. But there are volunteer opportunities suitable for every season of life.

The new volunteers are breaking many of the traditional volunteer stereotypes. They are senior citizens, middle-aged workers and professionals, high-school students, families, kids, young parents, or single adults in their thirties and forties.

Volunteering can be immensely rewarding—if you can find the right opportunity. Understanding how the seasons of life affect your contribution as a volunteer may help you in your quest. Like the government's unemployment statistics, our options for volunteering need to be seasonally adjusted. So let's consider how volunteering can fit in with the various seasons of your life.

MID-LIFE: CRISIS OR OPPORTUNITY?

Most researchers on aging consider forty-five to sixty years old middle-aged. Those of us who fall into that age group prefer to think of ourselves as approaching middle age. Middle age seems to be one of those seasons of life measured on a sliding scale: your current age plus five years.

In a national poll conducted for the American Board of Family Practice, one thousand two hundred Americans described some tell-tale markers of middle age. Middle age is that time of life when:

- You start to think more of the past than the future.
- You don't recognize the names of new popular music groups (Whatever happened to the Bee-Gees?).
- You take a day or two longer to recover from strenuous exercise.[1]

For all the discussion of the mid-life crisis, there is growing evidence that mid-life is a time of new opportunity and strengthened values—opportunities and values that mark middle age as prime time for volunteering. As reported in the New York Times, "researchers are finding that for many, middle age is the most fruitful phase of life, a time when intense preoccupations with marriage and career have faded and the inevitable deterioration of the body is yet to come.... while there is a reordering of priorities for most people in their forties and fifties, that reassessment often leads to a more compassionate attitude, a richer emotional life, and a deepening of relationships."[2]

The same article noted several studies which show that altruism—the concern for others—increases significantly as people enter the mid-life years. According to Dr. George E. Valliant, "You find people doing things at forty-five they just weren't bothering with before, getting more concerned about other people. As one man put it, in my twenties I learned to get along with my wife, in my thirties to get ahead in my job. In my forties I worried about other people's lives."[3]

Quoting David Holmes, a psychologist at the University of Kansas, the article notes how men and women tend to experience the opportunities of middle age differently. "Women say the happiest period of their lives is when their children grow up and leave home. It opens up all kinds of possibilities for them; they report being more mellow, and yet more assertive. For men in their forties, though, the big change is that they discover relationships. They turn from a focus on their careers to one that includes the people in their lives; they want both."[4]

The article reports similar findings from Dr. Robert Michels, chairman of the psychiatry department at Cornell Medical School. "If people are reasonably mature in middle age, they no longer experience their ideals and ambitions in a limited personal sense, but in a larger perspective. They are less concerned with their own striving, and more interested in the meaning of their lives and in touching the lives around them."[5]

Dan and Bev Heffernan, mid-lifers from the midwest, are living proof of the new research on middle age. Dan established a successful family medical practice and together with Bev raised six children. Dan became increasingly concerned about the impact of the health care crisis on the poor. He watched as many of his colleagues were forced by economic pressures to limit their care of Medicaid patients. The state-sponsored safety net was riddled with gaping holes.

Dan and Bev responded by offering free medical care in a poor neighborhood every Saturday. Dan provided the clinical skills and Bev gave strong nurturing and organizational abilities—and, most of all, her time—to help the people who came to the clinic with many other needs. Inspired by their example, others began to volunteer their time, giving birth to what has now become Hope Medical Clinic. They provide food, clothing, and personal support to the poor throughout the week—all based on the person-to-person model of neighbors helping neighbors in need. The core of volunteers are people like Dan and Bev—mid-lifers with a desire to touch the lives of those in need.

Nancy is another woman in her middle years who has found deep satisfaction in helping others. With her children either married or off to school, Nancy knew that this was her opportunity to expand her horizons. She volunteered once a week at the Pregnancy Counseling Center where she brought her listening skills and her experience of bearing children to women facing crisis pregnancies. Nancy became a combination friend and older mom to frightened young mothers-to-be, giving her own special brand of personal attention to each one. She helped to arrange obstetrical care, free clothing, and sometimes even housing. She has several pictures at home of babies whose births were facilitated because she was there to lend a hand at a critical time.

MID-MENTORS

Those who give their time in middle age to help others are often drawn to mentoring roles. A mentor is someone who has been there before, someone who acts as personal coach, often to a younger person. The professional baseball player who becomes a coach, the accountant who helps those deep in debt to manage their money, the experienced mom who helps new mothers, the "big brother" who takes a young person under his wing—all are examples of mentors. This is an ideal volunteer role for those in middle age because it takes advantage of the volunteer's life experience and skills and combines these with the mid-life instinct to pass on what has been gained to a younger generation.

And for the middle-aged man who feels a need for investing more in relationships after many years of devotion to more functional tasks, mentoring provides an excellent opportunity. Scott is an African-American who, along with other men like himself, has worked with young people in his community who need the guidance of an older person. He's commented to me about what a satisfying experience it's been for him and other men, mentoring elementary-school-age boys.

What has made Scott and others feel so good is the relationship they have built with the boys at Baille and Jones Schools. Fewer than half have fathers living in the home and many lack any male role model, such as a grandfather or older brother. They seem to crave the attention of strong, caring males.

"I feel like they're my godfathers," said one fifth grader at Baille Elementary. "They changed me because I used to fight a lot and now I don't. I brought my grades up from C's to B's to A's and B's."[6]

THE SENIOR ADVANTAGE

The senior years are years of advantage for those who volunteer. Erik Erikson has described the need for men and women in their older years to transfer values, culture, and knowledge gained to a younger generation—the need for "generativity."[7]

This need was often met through the family, but increased mobility in our society has often meant decreased opportunities for senior citizens to have contact with their grandchildren. Many children are not growing up with the anchoring influence of a grandparent figure. Volunteering provides an opportunity for seniors and young people to develop those vitally important relationships—relationships where "Helping you is helping me."

Helene and Stanley volunteer one morning each week at the local elementary school's breakfast program for children from low-income families. As the retired couple helps serve the breakfast, they are assuming a familial, rather than an institutional, role.

They may talk with a child about last night's frightening dream or the activities planned for the new day. A little girl may show Helene the tooth she lost over the weekend or ask Stanley if he could help fix a favorite doll.

"We look forward to our breakfast morning," says Helene. "Time goes so fast. And this keeps you young... I seem to be grandma to everyone, in church and here." For Helene and Stanley, it is a manageable task; they can make a real contribution without returning to the stresses of full-time parenting. And for the children, the regular weekly contact provides so much more than breakfast.

Many people discover the joys of volunteering as seniors. Bill, from Marietta, Georgia, tells his story.

The year was 1942 and there was a war on. I was at Fort Des Moines, Iowa. At my first roll call, the army's version of Arnold Schwarzenegger lined us up and bellowed, "All experienced truck drivers two steps forward!" I had driven large farm trucks.

I knew all about "super-low" and "double-clutching" so I gladly volunteered. Besides, driving a truck seemed like pretty good duty in the Army. The officer looked pleased as seven of us stepped forward. "Fine," he roared. "Now truck on down to the mess hall. You seven fools are on K.P.!"

Unfortunately, I never forgot that graphic lesson and I was sixty-eight years old before I volunteered for anything significant again. Even then, I doubted my sanity, but the Lord was leading and I didn't dare hold back. One evening in October of 1986, I came with my wife to a church conference. The speaker was a powerfully built, bearded man who used a cane to walk, but was so full of the Spirit that I wonder he didn't fly!

The speaker shared with us some simple but shattering experiences of directly meeting desperate human needs. Workers were few, worthy clients were many, and the help of people like myself was needed. A few days later, surprising no one more than myself, I stepped forward to volunteer my help. But this time, the joke was not on me. I felt that I was a man of unclean motives among a people of questionable priorities, but I had received a vision. I saw the Lord as an almost solitary figure in the harvest field of human hurt and heard him say "Who can I send?" Along with many others, I answered, "Here I am, send me!"[8]

I have an older friend named Stan, who, like Bill felt the tug to volunteer late in life. A vigorous retiree in his seventies, Stan is an avid golfer. Along with some of his golfing buddies he signed up to sponsor a handicapped man in a Special Olympics Golf Scramble.

With two of his friends, Stan took Jim, a fifty-eight-year-old stroke victim, who had lost most of his speech and social abilities, through a round of golf. When Jim became confused out on the course, the others didn't know what to do so they pretended not to notice. But Stan stepped forward, took Jim by the hand, and led him through the remaining holes—speaking words of reassurance and encouragement along the way.

For the rest of the evening, Stan had a fast friend in Jim. He took him out to dinner, helping him throughout the evening. Stan's friends were amazed at how he cared for Jim. "We didn't know what to do, but you stepped right in there!"

Stan told me that when he returned home that night, he cried for the first time in years. He was overcome with a sense of his own good fortune, of all the things he had come to take for granted. He was reminded of his own father, who had gone through a period of disability. And he vowed to make the Special Olympics Golf Scramble a regular part of his life.

Part of the shock that comes with retirement is the realization that several of these needs are met on the job. Too often, retirement from work leads to a loss of human connections.

Before you get the golden watch...

If you are a senior and planning for retirement, you may want to ask yourself, which of my basic needs are being met at work? How will they be filled when I retire?

In a poll conducted by George Gallup, Jr., seven needs of the average American were identified:

1. The need for shelter and food.
2. The need to believe life is meaningful and has a purpose.
3. The need for a sense of community and deeper relationships.
4. The need to be appreciated and respected.
5. The need to be listened to and be heard.
6. The need to feel one is growing in faith.
7. The need for practical help in developing a mature faith.[9]

Ironically, this occurs at time when the need for human interaction and the potential for giving is greatest. So if you are approaching retirement without a specific volunteer opportunity in mind, give this some serious thought. By all means, make a second human connection, a meaningful link with others who need you before you sever the connection at work. And if you have some older friends or parents in this season of life, suggest that they consider the senior advantage.

VOLUNTEERING IS FOR KIDS TOO

The youngest generation of Americans will inherit a host of social problems. With the burden of our national debt inhibiting the response of government to these ills, the needs of this generation will land even more squarely on the shoulders of volunteers. We must be sure that they also inherit an optimistic, "can-do" spirit which makes caring as natural and inevitable as breathing. Introducing children and young people to the joys of helping others is a crucial task.

By many accounts, the kids are eager—with the right help—to get into the fray. In churches, schools, and families around the country, we are seeing a new generation of volunteers step forward. Melissa leads a group of junior and senior high students at her church. When asked what makes for effective Bible study with this age group, Melissa didn't hesitate: "They want to study the Bible in conjunction with *doing* something meaningful. Like last month, when we prepared a meal for the Sunday dinner our church puts on for the homeless. Afterwards, we discussed the passage where Jesus says, 'When I was hungry, you gave me something to eat; when I was naked, you clothed me.' It was one of the best Bible studies we ever had, because they were directly involved in what the Bible was talking about."

From the same church, Mr. Kelsey's fifth and sixth grade Sunday school class was talking about a recent hurricane disaster and how Jesus would want to help the people who were struggling to rebuild their lives in the storm's aftermath. The television images of families with roofless homes had left quite an impression on the kids, and they wanted to do something. So they held a worship-while-we-wash car wash during the next Sunday service, receiving donations to be sent to the Salvation Army hurricane relief effort.

For a generation raised in the era of television ministry scandals, understanding that faith is more than talk is essential. What better way to learn than by doing? After all, that was Jesus' favorite method of teaching. He brought his friends along with him as he reached out to the poor, sick, and needy. It was the most effective way to pass on his values.

A CHILD'S PERSPECTIVE

Have you ever noticed how a child feels that no injury is so severe that a kiss will not make it better? I was reminded of that when my two-year-old daughter responded to the news that Grandma Jessie, our ninety-two-year-old friend, had a serious hearing problem. "I'll kiss it and make it better," Laura asserted with every confidence that her kiss would do just that.

Laura's four-year-old sister, Emily, had a more practical solution. Advised that we would have to speak quite loudly because of Jessie's severe hearing deficit, Emily positioned herself next to Jessie and proceeded to literally yell in Jessie's ear. It was a little unnerving for those of us with good hearing. But as Emily's high-pitched voice penetrated the silence of Jessie's deafness, she broke into a smile that grew brighter as she heard the evidence of a little girl's love.

As important as volunteering is for kids, it is also important not to idealize or romanticize the process—as we are sometimes tempted to do with anything involving children. Children need good supervision and preparation in order to avoid a negative experience. Children are like the rest of us, only more so! They are especially vulnerable to fear in different volunteer situations.

For example, children can make a unique contribution in activities like visiting the elderly in nursing homes. For many older people, the sight of a young face is immensely refreshing and encouraging. But if children are their usual rambunctious selves, they can disturb nursing home patients as easily as they can delight them. So proper supervision is a must for the safety of all concerned.

Similarly, some children can be frightened by any setting that is unfamiliar or by the sight of people with serious medical problems. Rather than bring a younger child into a lounge full of nursing home patients, it is better to begin with something more manageable—a visit to a patient's room, for example, to familiarize the child with new surroundings. Talk with the child beforehand to prepare him or her for any new sights and discuss the visit afterwards. Remember, older children and teens might be embarrassed to voice their fears, but like the rest of us, they have them.

A FAMILY AFFAIR

According to a recent report on family volunteerism conducted by the W.K. Kellogg Foundation and the Points of Light Foundation, "There are two major reasons that families from all ethnic groups with different income levels volunteer in their communities. The first: desire to pass along values of service for others and their communities to the next generation. The second: to strengthen family bonds through volunteering as a group."[10]

One of the best ways to involve children in volunteering is by choosing activities that allow for family involvement. Nine-year-old Sandy accompanied her father when he responded to a church request to fix an elderly man's stove. Once Sandy saw the situation, she turned to her dad and said, "This man isn't as lazy as we thought he would be." Sandy suggested that her Dad mow the gentleman's grass, which was badly needed. Sandy's mom was irritated by how long the excursion took, but was soon humbled by her daughter's account of the man's need and how much the help meant to him.

More bridge organizations that facilitate volunteering are providing these opportunities. A volunteer center in Orange County, California, launched a program called Family Helping Hands. One of their projects is to bring families into the fertile fields of Orange County to glean fresh fruits and vegetables after the harvest.

Even young children are able to help in gleaning for some crops. And the results are plain for all to see, young and old alike, as fresh produce is gathered to supplement the supplies of soup kitchens and homeless shelters, which tend to rely on dry and canned goods.

What's good for the poor is also good for the families. "Just look at these kids rooting around in the dirt," observes Charlene Tuco of Irvine. "The younger ones may not know what they're doing this for," she says, stooping over a row of beans while her husband and son work nearby rows, "but they're here with their moms and dads. They're here as a family. I think they leave with an appreciation that there are things you can do as a family."

"For the older children, the sight of mom or dad hunkered down in a field of beans so someone else can eat better is a powerful lesson that can't be learned from all the tax-deductible charitable contributions in the world," Jim Turco adds.[11]

For over fourteen years the Rainos family has deepened their family ties as they served other families in the Chicago Uptown Ministry. It began when daughter Julie volunteered as a helper in the pre-school morning program. Julie brought her work home: in this case, four-year-old Clara, whose mother was hospitalized for an extended period. Soon Julie's parents were sharing their talents with other families. Mom helped launch a church-based nurse program. Dad offered his construction skills (and fatherly advice) to several families. Other sisters helped organize special events. Grown up now, the Rainos daughters, who learned the satisfactions of volunteering in their family, continue the tradition in their own families.

Isn't that what so many of us would long to do? To encounter a manageable need which serves as the first step to a personal encounter, an experience so rich that we share it with those most important to us—the members of our own families.

THE THING TO DO

Did you realize that teenagers volunteer more than adults do? The Independent Sector Report found that in 1989, 58 percent of teens volunteered compared with 54 percent of adults. These young people averaged nearly four hours per week in volunteer activities. Most of these efforts occurred in the school setting.[12]

In fact, a new strategy for involving student volunteers selects those who are considered at high risk for dropping out of school. A study reported in the summer 1991 issues of *The*

Journal of Volunteer Administration found that volunteering helped these students change and improve their attitudes toward their own futures. The student volunteers—selected by criteria based on poverty level, poor attendance, low grades and so on—were matched with a latchkey child in elementary school. Working in closely supervised groups, the older students coached the younger ones in safety techniques. The younger students identified with the older ones who responded positively because they were being taken seriously, often for the first time.[13]

THE SINGLE ADVANTAGE

An increasing percentage of Americans are single. For some, singleness is a chosen lifestyle; for others, the result of divorce, the loss of a spouse, or simply the delay of marriage. But singleness can provide distinct advantages when it comes to volunteering.

Lynn managed a successful medical practice for several years, generating a comfortable income. But she felt an insistent tug to help people who are on the fringe of society. For all her sophistication, Lynn came from a colorful background, describing her stint as a "motorcycle mama." Now she felt a strong desire to help people from a similar background.

Lynn bought a house in a middle-class neighborhood that bordered on a poorer section of her hometown. With the support of her church and with careful screening of individuals, Lynn has been able to open her home for periods of a few days to a few months to women in need—a place to stay while they get their feet on the ground.

While singleness has its own set of challenges, it affords some real advantages too—flexibility, availability, and the opportunity to focus on those beyond the immediate family. These and other advantages can be realized in helping others.

Single people beyond the college years often have a need for relationships beyond the friendships and associations that develop through work. The person-to-person helping relationships advocated in this book may be especially important for the single volunteer, in particular, opportunities for relationships with people that one doesn't ordinarily meet in the work place—the elderly, children, and teens. Single volunteers may also want to select options that include the chance to work with other volunteers.

HOMEMAKERS

Homemakers often underestimate what they have to offer as volunteers. They can often run rings around others with their combination of organizational abilities and compassionate love.

Elaine is a mother who offered her unconditional love in spite of the ill-founded warnings of others. Elaine was asked by her church in Fairbanks, Alaska, to provide Jean, a homeless woman who some feared was mentally ill, with personal items like soap and shampoo. After getting to know Jean better, Elaine went beyond the original request and invited Jean to her home for a visit. She washed Jean's clothes, lovingly persuaded her to bathe and then applied medication to kill the lice. She cooked her a meal and listened to her stories.

Elaine also invited Jean to return whenever she wished. Jean did so—frequently. Though Jean moved away when colder weather set in, she still kept in touch with Elaine, who had become someone of inestimable value to Jean, a friend.

Mariel began her volunteer involvement with pre-school moms in Chicago when she was nearing the end of her first pregnancy. Mariel, an American Indian, led a group of other Indians, African-Americans, and Mexican-Americans in working with colorful yarn. Besides tapping many of their creative talents, she was able to spark a valuable discussion as the other mothers shared their hard-earned parenting lessons with each other. Mariel is sure she experienced at least as much love and support as she gave in that group; the distinction between helper and those helped blurred as it so often does.

Because of the unique demands placed on homemakers, volunteer opportunities need to be flexible. Options that allow a homemaker to include volunteer service with the ongoing activities of life may work best: picking up a few groceries for an elderly neighbor along with one's own shopping, calling a lonely person during a child's nap time, supporting a new mother by phone contact.

For homemakers who have the opportunity to get out of the house and leave the kids behind with a babysitter for a few hours, a volunteer position more like a regular job may be a refreshing change of pace. For example, exchanging babysitting with other volunteer homemakers is one option for the ever-challenging babysitting problem.

Volunteers in a volunteer-friendly organization can provide some of the elements often lacking in a homemaker's home-based work experience. Projects that can actually be completed and measured—unlike the long-term task of raising children—may be a welcome change of pace to the unique stresses of the homemaker's role.

VOLUNTEERING: A DYNAMIC PROCESS

Matching volunteer opportunities to fit your season of life is a dynamic process. Helping others is a lifestyle that works its way out at different times in your life. There may well be certain seasons of your life when helping others through volunteering must take a back seat to other concerns. But before you discount your ability to make a difference now, think creatively about the wide variety of volunteer opportunities. Don't focus on what you can't do. Consider what you can. Chances are you will be able to make a difference for others, even when you least expect it.

NINE

Avoiding the Potholes

Perhaps you live in Southern California or some other temperate clime; but here in the intemperate Midwest, the roads are full of potholes, craters of varying sizes that mark the highway landscape. Especially at night, you can be driving along without a care in the world. Then, bam! You've slammed into a pothole. Potholes have been known to provoke streams of profanity from some of the nicest people. Potholes make driving an adventure.

There are some common difficulties that most volunteers encounter sooner or later. Like potholes on the highway they can ruin your day, but if you know what to look out for, many can be avoided.

FACING VOLUNTEER FEAR

It is entirely normal to feel nervous, anxious, or even frightened about the volunteer experience facing you. In fact, this is a good sign since it indicates an understanding of the importance of the venture you are about to undertake. In a television interview with Billy Graham, who has probably addressed more people than anyone alive, Diane Sawyer asked, "Do you still get nervous when you speak?" His answer probably surprised more viewers than just me: "Yes, I sure do. In fact, I'm nervous here speaking with you."[1]

Granted, public speaking isn't pleasant when the notes in your hand shake from fear and your voice takes on the eerie quality of a strangling victim trying to call for help. But the sense of anticipation or nervousness in reasonable measure actually helps a speaker to be more alert and focused. Those who speak regularly get really worried when they don't feel any nervousness at all.

Understanding the source of our fear may not remove it completely—it rarely does—but it does temper the power of fear to paralyze us. When we volunteer to help other people in serious need, our fears often take one of three forms.

FEAR OF THE UNKNOWN

Most of us thrive on the familiar. We like the unexpected twist in our mystery novels, but we want daily life to be more predictable. Just enough of the unknown to keep life interesting but not too much, thank you. Most volunteer experiences bring us beyond our comfort zones. At first, we find ourselves relating to people who are not a familiar part of our landscape, or we find ourselves in situations that contain elements of the unknown.

Think about a relatively low-risk first volunteer experience: helping to serve a meal to the homeless in the Salvation Army soup kitchen. It's not like jumping out of an airplane, or solo white-water rafting. But it probably brings you into unfamiliar territory. The soup kitchen may be located in a part of town that's new to you. The people who come as guests may not remind you of your co-workers, that is, until you get to know them. These two factors alone will stimulate at least a mild form of nervousness.

But there is a bright side to the fear of the unknown. It

doesn't last long. It may seem an imposing fear at first glance, but its bark is far worse than its bite. Most people who serve a meal to the homeless will begin by feeling mildly apprehensive; some may feel downright frightened; but they force themselves to dive in anyway. But after one experience, they come away saying things like this:

"Gee, that wasn't so bad, after all!"

"Once you get into it, it's kind of fun."

"Some of the people looked unusual, and a few acted pretty strange, but on the whole they seemed like regular folks."

"These people are a lot like us."

The dynamics of any new social situation apply to a new volunteer experience. It's not that different from going to your first class in a new school, or your first Christmas party at a new job. At first, you feel a little out of place. You exchange pleasantries with the nearest friendly face and move on to get something to drink so as not to press your luck. By the end of the evening, you're starting to think, "This isn't so bad!"

The fear of the unknown is probably the easiest fear to conquer because time and experience transform the unknown to the familiar, defanging the fear. All it takes is that initial willingness to walk through the door when you suddenly feel like doing something else—anything else, as a matter of fact.

Of course some of the fear you may face as a volunteer stemming from the fear of the unknown will take longer to deal with. The fear of an unfamiliar setting is easier to handle than the fear of unfamiliar people. More challenging still is the fear of people in circumstances completely outside of your experience. If you've never visited a relative with a terminal disease or sat with someone dying in a hospital room, you will have more fear to overcome as a hospice volunteer. But time and experience will temper even this fear of the unknown.

THE FEAR OF POVERTY

Most of us are afraid of being poor. My mother, who was raised during the Great Depression, always kept her kitchen cupboards full of food and a closet downstairs too. It was her way of handling the fear of returning to the poverty of those days. Perhaps the fear of poverty is just another manifestation of that mother of all fears, the fear of death. After all, poverty, if it's severe enough, threatens our very existence.

Encountering poor people is a painful reminder that poverty is a real threat. Being with poor people may trigger this fear in us—especially if we consider ourselves providers. What would happen if I lost my job? What would happen if I became disabled and the insurance money ran out? What if we face another severe depression when people previously immune to poverty become poor?

While facing the fear of poverty through a volunteer experience may touch this tender spot of fear, it can also help us to deal with the fear by facing it head on. Many times this fear has surfaced in me while helping someone in need. That's when I've been pressed to activate my faith in a God who cares about me and provides for me.

After all we can't really avoid these kinds of fears, whether the fear of sickness, poverty, or death. We can avoid all the painful reminders and still be enslaved to the fear. It might display itself in constant worry over our jobs or a drive to accumulate wealth that is never satisfied. Better to face these things directly if that can drive us to a more firmly held faith.

THE FEAR OF INADEQUACY

Consider some of the most pressing needs that call for us to help our neighbors: AIDS, the needs of single parents in poverty, high-school students facing powerful pressures to drop out, babies of mothers addicted to crack. Who wouldn't feel inadequate in the face of problems like these? Little wonder, then, that those who lend a hand to neighbors with these kinds of needs struggle with the fear of inadequacy.

Part of this fear is grounded in a misperception of the volunteer's role. When it comes to people helping other people, we are profoundly influenced by the professional model. This model imposes certain expectations on those who offer help to others. A helper in the professional model is someone who has become an expert, having mastered a field of study—whether dentistry, medicine, law, psychology, or social work. The professional relationship is a one-way relationship in which the professional with superior knowledge and skill in a particular field helps someone else. The professional model doesn't encourage friendships, but a cordial distance. It's a sad fact that much of the training given to physicians on relating well to patients is designed to prevent litigation.

The professional model is probably the dominant model for people helping other people in our society. So it is easy for volunteers to feel that they must in some sense be the experts in a helping relationship. While many people are inclined to volunteer their professional services—for example, a lawyer volunteers his legal expertise to a poor client—most volunteers are simply neighbors helping other neighbors. They are not professionals serving patients, clients, or customers.

A volunteer who is helping someone struggling with mental illness doesn't provide diagnosis, treatment, or therapy, but friendship—a listening ear, a helping hand, a personal presence. A volunteer who serves as a mentor to a high-school student isn't a professional educator. The volunteer is like a caring aunt or uncle who shows a personal interest in the young person—someone who cares, not someone who provides a service.

Do you see how this takes the rug out from under much of our feelings of inadequacy? In most volunteer roles, you don't have to be the expert with all the answers. In many situations that would be counterproductive. What's needed is a neighbor, a friend, a caring individual.

OVERCOMING VOLUNTEER FEAR

No matter what the source of your volunteer fear, most fears can be managed and minimized. Good training from a more experienced helper is one of the best antidotes to fear.

Most volunteer experiences can be broken down to manageable steps. Effective training helps us to walk through a new experience one step at a time. Let's return to the person who wants to help feed the homeless in a soup kitchen setting. Even this relatively simple task can be broken down into smaller steps.

For example, before showing up at meal time, you can visit the soup kitchen when no guests are present, just to familiarize yourself with the surroundings. An experienced volunteer can sit down with you and go over the experience from start to finish. Next, you can go help out in the kitchen preparing the food. If you're not good in the kitchen, you can be the "go-fer" and the person to clean up the counters as others do the cooking.

The next time you volunteer, you can help serve the food. Working together with someone who has done it before, you watch and learn as you do some simple task. Someone is nearby to answer any questions you have. Before long, you will get to know some of the guests, and you will be comfortable sitting down with them to talk once the meal is served. You will have bridged an invisible barrier, step by step. Next week, you'll be showing some nervous newcomer how it's done.

There are very few volunteer opportunities that don't lend themselves to the following simple progression of involvement:

1. Talk with someone who has done it before.
2. Go with someone experienced and observe that person in action.
4. Go with someone and assist him or her.
5. Go with someone and do the task while the more experienced person is available to help out if needed.
6. Go and do the task yourself, with phone number to call if you run into trouble.
7. Take someone along with you who needs to be trained!

The process might take five minutes, five weeks, or five months, but it is guaranteed to cut your fear down to a manageable size.

HELPING THE UNGRATEFUL

I ran into this second volunteer pothole while delivering food to a family of four during a lull in a horrendous Michigan snowstorm. My fiancée came with me to the house in her front-wheel drive car. As we approached the house, a young mother opened the door, pointed to the kitchen table, and whispered a barely audible thanks as she escorted us out of the house as quickly as we came in. Her husband sat at the table. He watched our every move but said nothing and made no attempt to help us.

My fiancée and I were quiet as we slipped down the road. When she finally spoke, the feelings were mine: "They sure didn't seem very grateful, did they?"

No, they didn't express much gratitude. But experiences like this have helped me understand a few things: my own reasons for helping, the factors behind people's lack of expressed thanks, and the different ways people express their gratitude.

THE HELPING MOTIVE

It's easy to get involved in volunteerism because we want to have our needs met. We see in the volunteer experience a way to find the affirmation that is so elusive in other parts of our lives. In recent years, I have seen this tendency expressed following both the earthquake in Oakland, California, and the riots in Los Angeles. My work in those settings in the days immediately following the disasters was frustrating precisely because certain helpers demanded more attention than the victims did.

For example, one man called the disaster relief center in Los Angeles with an unusual request. He was ready to help someone and he wanted it to be the man wearing the yellow jacket.

"The yellow jacket?" the telephone volunteer asked.

"Yes. You know. He was on all the television reports. If you give me his name and address, I'll help him."

Perhaps helping the man in the yellow jacket would have made the man feel good, but it would have taken needless hours of research to locate the man in the yellow jacket!

When we find ourselves bothered by people's lack of expressed gratitude—and we will—it's time to consider again our motives for helping. Are we helping simply to secure some short-term benefit? Those benefits are real, and they encourage us in the right direction; but if they are the bottom line for our volunteering, we may find ourselves frustrated.

Perhaps you remember the story of Jesus healing the ten lepers. After the lepers where healed, they took off without a word of thanks—all except one. Even when Jesus did something dramatic he ran into the phenomenon of ingratitude. Ten lepers healed, yet only one returns to give thanks. Perhaps the percentages hold in our efforts to help others. For every person who expresses thanks, there may be nine who don't bother.

While the lack of expressed thanks was sad to see, it didn't prevent Jesus from helping others just like them. Jesus was motivated to help others for deeper reasons than the immediate reward of gratitude from those he served. He helped them because he wanted to. He helped them because he knew that they were of immense value in the eyes of God even if they didn't know that themselves.

WHY PEOPLE DON'T SAY THANKS

Many people who receive help are silenced by their own sense of shame. A proud husband who feels like a failure because his family has been reduced to needing charity may find it difficult to accept help and difficult to give thanks when it is given. People in need, especially those experiencing need for the first time, may receive help with the greatest reluctance. They're not good at it and they don't know how to respond. Like many of us, they are far better at giving help than receiving it.

On the other hand, the director of a rescue mission in Los Angeles tells me that chronically dependent people, many of them damaged by years of life on the street, are touched by compassion only when they see it offered to a third person. They fail to respond when receiving help themselves because they view that as their role in life. But their responses change when they see a volunteer provide assistance to another needy person.

READING BETWEEN THE LINES

Some people are so emotionally impoverished that they don't know how to express thanks to another human being. They may express their gratitude in code form. Perhaps they will remember your name next time they see you or ask about your health. They may look you in the eye and smile, reach out and touch your arm, or tell you their favorite worn-out joke.

One volunteer was helping acclimate a new family from Latin America to North American-style baking. She took the two daughters out for a trip to the grocery store to buy ingredients for chocolate chip cookies. "We returned to my house to bake, which was all new to the girls. Following directions in English was also new. Soon the house was filled with good smells and they were asking questions about my house, our hobbies, and my children. After the baking was completed, the girls counted all the cookies. They asked how many family members I had and counted out a matching stack of cookies. They did the same for my friend who had come to help us. 'These are to give,' they said proudly together. The rest went home to their family." This was a more powerful expression of thanks than any words could express.

Sometimes those who are helped don't feel comfortable saying thanks directly to the volunteer, but they may express gratitude to a third party. It's wonderful when these reports filter back to you. Charlene was helping a very troubled young woman named Sue Ann, who said little to Charlene about the impact of her help, but shared the following perspective with the bridge organization that linked them together.

> All of my life I felt on the outside. I wasn't good enough for my parents, and it was like everyone else could see that.
>
> Kids made fun of me. Parents were even worse. They were always polite. You know, they would say nice things, but they didn't want their kids being friends with me. It was like there was this club that everyone belonged to but me, and I could never get in. I guess I didn't care anymore.
>
> Finally someone from a neighborhood church told me God loves me, and I should ask him into my life. I did and he really came. That blows my mind. I mean, I'm not a very good person. You have to mess up pretty bad to have your kids taken away like I did. But he took me. I mean, that's hard to believe. The thing that really got me was Charlene's bringing me to church and being a friend to me. And it wasn't like I fooled her. She knew all the stuff I'd done, and she still wants to be my friend.

A report like that can keep a volunteer going for a long time.

FOOLS RUSH IN

A third challenge to those who are volunteering to help others comes in the form of a powerful temptation: the desire to rush in and fix the problems like an appliance repairman.

Joy is a college student at New York University who gains great satisfaction from her volunteer work. She began to work with Rob, a recovering alcoholic and drug addict who was a new Christian. Rob's finances were in shambles; several of his close relationships were a mess. He had a terrible work record and his current employer was upset by his lack of follow-through.

Full of youthful enthusiasm, Joy saw herself as the answer to Rob's problems. She would get him back on the path of financial sanity, help him repair damaged relationships, and coach him to handle his duties at work without alienating another boss.

He was too stubborn to let an enthusiastic young person take over as a surrogate parent. At first, Joy was frustrated. If only Rob would listen to her good advice, he could get his life back together! But she began to realize that she didn't have all the answers and that people like Rob cannot rebuild their lives over a few months' time. People need time and space to change, not an answer man to tell them what to do.

Eventually Joy began to see Rob from a different perspective. He wasn't a challenge, but a person in progress. She allowed him to take responsibility for his own life, leaving the work of transformation to God.

Erica told the volunteer coordinator of the grade-school mentoring program about her brush with the Mr. Fix-it mentality. Erica's first meeting with a third-grader named Alice had been exciting. They went to the library together, where Erica showed her how to find books and check them out. They read together and Alice got her first library card. At their next time together, Alice was in the same clothes she had worn before; but they were much dirtier this time. Her face was dirty, and she was in need of a good bath.

"I just wanted to take her to the bathroom and clean her up," Erica told the volunteer coordinator. "But then I decided to wait and really get to know Alice and her family first. I don't want Alice to be ashamed or shy about meeting with me and I don't want to anger her parents."

Erica had just passed one of the toughest tests of a volunteer. She was learning to go slow in encouraging change and she realized that change should not come at the expense of an individual's sense of dignity.

LOVING THOSE WHO DON'T GET FIXED

Often we get to love to people who don't change—at least not as we would like them to. Jeff tells about his relationship with Mike.

My friend Mike lives in a home for mentally disabled people near our ministry center in downtown Denver. Because Mike is six-feet-six-inches tall, wears a heavy down jacket every day of the year—summer included—and places personal hygiene low on his list of priorities, he makes his presence known. I run into him almost every day, and he always asks me for forty cents. Whether I give it to him or not, Mike always gives me a big smile and says, "Jeff, you're really Ron Eli, aren't you—the guy who played Tarzan in the movies? You look just like him!"

Not many days go by when we don't rehearse that scene. Sometimes it brightens my day and sometimes it's a bother. One snowy day as I was crossing the street on my way to buy cup of coffee at the 7-Eleven I saw Mike headed my way. I wanted to avoid him, but instead, I heard that still small voice urging me to take the initiative this time and offer to buy Mike something for Mike. So as we stood together at the counter I said, "Hey Mike! Get whatever you like... my treat!" Mike took me up on the offer, selecting a package of beef jerky for $3.89. A surprise move, because he was standing in front of the donuts when I made my offer. "You said I could get whatever I wanted," Mike said with a larger than usual grin on his face. Then he added, "Jeff, you're really Ron Eli, aren't you? You know, the guy who plays Tarzan in the movies. You look just like him!"

People like Mike remind us that God's love is a gift, plain and simple.

HELPING DIFFICULT PEOPLE

One of the reasons some people are reluctant to teach Sunday school, coach a peewee baseball team, or work with a group of kids, is the prospect of handling the proverbial problem child. He or she is the one uncooperative, demanding, and disruptive child who seems to dominate everything and everyone. The fear of this one child is enough to scare away even those most gifted and motivated to work with children.

Volunteers who value the people-helping-people approach can be derailed by one demanding and manipulative individual who makes helping others a purgatorial pursuit. Some think that adopting the helping role means putting yourself at the mercy of the demanding individual. But it's just not so.

The most caring, generous and effective volunteers are those who have learned how to respond to the individual who seems so hard to love. Here's a few tips that may help you to help one of those hard to love people.

1. Know your limits. A church volunteer was asked to drive the wife of a prisoner to a visit at the prison. The volunteer drove to Sherry's apartment to pick her up. When Sherry got into the car she turned to the volunteer and said, "You're aware of your responsibilities, aren't you?"

"Yes, I think so," the volunteer replied. "I'm here to take you to the prison to see your husband."

"That's right," Sherry responded with an air of authority. "And you need to help me look good for the visit. So let's go shopping for a dress you can buy for me."

The volunteer was caught off guard by Sherry's confidence. She came with the intention of helping and she didn't want to start by refusing a request. Maybe it was part of her responsibilities and no one remembered to tell her. At any rate, she did as Sherry asked. But it didn't feel right and the volunteer only felt the resentment of someone who has been manipulated afterwards.

The volunteer didn't have a good grasp of her volunteer

responsibilities. She didn't have a clear understanding of her limits. If she had, she could have told Sherry, "I'm afraid I can't buy you a dress, but I can provide transportation to the prison for you. Do you still want to go, or should we arrange another time?"

Knowing your limits and making those limits plain is especially important when helping demanding individuals. The authoritative, demanding nature of Sherry's request was probably a symptom of a manipulative strategy. A small group of people adopt this approach to helping organizations. They are used to working the system. Some will continue to make demands until they discover the limits—usually in the form of a polite but firm no.

Knowing your limits—and making them clear—is just as important in helping people with needs that go beyond your ability to fulfill. Sometimes people are so starved for attention that they make demands on your time that you are not able to fulfill. Perhaps you are in touch with a lonely elderly person who would love to talk for hours on the phone. If you let the conversation go beyond your ability to cope—whether in terms of time or your emotional reserves—you will probably end up avoiding the person altogether. Far better to end the conversation when you need to go with a simple, "Mrs. Swanson, I'd love to be able to talk longer, but I have to go now. I'll plan to call you next week, OK?"

2. Don't be a martyr. Don't try to help someone if you are not equipped for the task. If you are not equipped to handle violent or abusive behavior—and few of us are, except the police—don't.

Consider the setting for meeting with someone you don't know well. It is safest to meet in a more public area—perhaps a restaurant—with other people around. Move away from the situation when you feel unable to handle it.

3. Don't hesitate to admit that you don't know how to respond to or advise someone. A dear friend of mine who has lived a very difficult life loves to pepper me with questions I don't know the answer to.

"Why is life so hard for me?"

"Why are things so unfair?"

"How am I going to get out of this mess?"

At first I felt uncomfortable because I didn't know how to respond. Then I heard myself saying, "I've wondered the same thing myself. That's a hard question that I don't have the answer to." I felt a great sense of relief. Loving the person did not mean answering his tough questions. It meant listening to his pain.

DEALING WITH DISCOURAGEMENT

No truly worthwhile venture—a marriage, building a home, establishing a new business, gaining an education, pursuing an athletic goal, raising children, rebuilding a car engine—is immune from the occasional experience of discouragement. It's part of every meaningful journey, including the adventure of helping others.

We've considered many of the primary sources of discouragement in this chapter: fears, lack of appreciation for your efforts, people who don't seem to benefit as much as you hoped, and those hard-to-love individuals. Discouragement is designed to get you out of the game, so you will need a strategy to fight back when it presses in on you.

1. Treasure the small successes. When the Jewish exiles who had returned from exile under the leadership of Ezra and Nehemiah faced discouragement, the prophet Zechariah came with words straight from heaven: "Do not despise the day of small beginnings." Those Jewish immigrants were involved in a noble venture, namely, rebuilding the walls of Jerusalem. Their neighbors were mocking their efforts, claiming that a few squirrels running along the rebuilt walls could knock them down. But the walls were being rebuilt—one stone at a time.

If you focus on what you haven't accomplished as a volunteer, you will give up. But if you focus on what you have accomplished with the grace of God, you will be strengthened to continue. Perhaps your relationship as a big brother hasn't revolutionized a young person's life, but you have been a voice to counter all the other voices that tell this young person that no one really cares. That's a contribution that shouldn't be despised. It's a small beginning, perhaps, but a beginning nonetheless. So when you evaluate your effectiveness, always put a premium on the question: What small but real contribution has been made?

2. Keep the pressure on God and off you. The pressure to redeem the world is not on your shoulders. That's God's responsibility. Your part is small—infinitesimal compared to his—but it is essential, because God has chosen to work through human beings like you and me. We all have small parts to play in the drama of God's grace, but the play is so wonderful that it's an honor to perform the least significant part in it. If we maintain a sense of our own littleness side by side with God's greatness, we will be less likely to let discouragement trip us up.

3. Employ the Buddy System. Sometimes freedom from discouragement is as close at hand as another volunteer who's been there and can give you a listening ear. That's why people who help others need to build relationship with others who can pick them up when they are down. Don't be a lone ranger, or a stand-in for Superman. Give someone a call when you are facing a tough challenge and tell that person about it. You may not always be able to solve your immediate problem, but you will feel better.

4. Build an encouragement file. Over a period of time as a volunteer, encouragement in various forms will come your way. Maybe a letter of appreciation from someone you helped. A colored picture straight from the heart of a young child. A note from a volunteer coordinator. A clipping from the newspaper describing how a project you are involved in is making a difference. I keep all of this stuff. It's in the top drawer of my dresser and the top drawer of my desk. Every now and then, I look it over. This is not an ego-trip, but a protection against discouragement.

You may want to keep a journal to include thoughts, impressions, comments from others that you find encouraging. Then when it seems that all your labor is in vain, read the journal for a fresh perspective,

ONE AT A TIME

Volunteering is an adventure. Like any adventure it promises excitement and satisfaction as well as the challenge of overcoming inevitable obstacles. Without the challenges, the excitement and satisfaction to be gained from helping others would be greatly diminished. That's why catching a trout from a mountain stream is more fulfilling than going to one of those trout farms where they hand you a pole with a piece of bacon on the hook and you drop it into a small pond packed with fish.

We've taken a whole chapter to review the most common problems volunteers may encounter. But remember, the challenges of volunteering come in manageable doses. You won't face all, or even most, in any given volunteer experience. Fortunately, just as you give help to individuals one at a time, so do the challenges arrive, one at a time.

TEN

When Enough Is Enough

JULY, 1972. I still remember my presumptuous prayer: "Lord, I'm ready for the ultimate challenge in helping prisoners." I didn't know what that challenge was. But I knew I was ready. After all, I was twenty-six years old, the proud owner of a doctorate from the University of Michigan, author of the first book on the subject of prison libraries, and the founder of libraries or educational programs in four jails and a federal prison.

Having earned my wings in prison work, I felt ready for a challenge worthy of my gifts. Without question, I could make a profound impact on the entire prison system, develop strategies that would humanize the experience of incarceration, and rehabilitate the captives. They needed me.

September, 1972. I was appointed Director of Inmate Education Programs at Genesee Community College in New York. I supervised inmates who were enrolled on campus as well as 100 inmate students at the notorious Attica Correctional Facility. Walking down Attica's long corridors, where the walls were pockmarked by bullets fired during the riots there, I told myself, "This is the challenge you've been looking for!" Famous last words.

February, 1973. The program had grown to 150 participants at Attica. We celebrated the graduation of six students—the first ceremony of its kind in the country. We had a three-person inmate staff for the college education program—another first. The Department of Health and Human Services named our project the most exemplary prison-based educational program at the college level in the nation.

But I didn't care. I didn't care about the program. I didn't care about the success. And remarkably, I didn't care any longer about the inmates.

I was experiencing full-blown burnout. Something more than fatigue or heavy stress. I'm talking about a system breakdown complete with a physician's encyclopedia of physical and emotional symptoms. These symptoms—a hypochondriac's worst nightmare—evolved into irrational fears. At one point, agoraphobia, the fear of open places, made it nearly impossible for me to leave the house.

I had never experienced anything remotely like this before. And I hope I never will again. Even now, I can vividly recall the sheer terror that came with parking my car in the prison lot. Gathering the courage to get out of the car, cross the parking lot, submit to a weapons search, and walk the half-mile of prison hallways to my office took every ounce of willpower I could muster. I had made that trip many times before without a second thought. But this was different because I was in burnout.

Sometimes I didn't make it out of the car, returning home instead. My body was drenched in sweat and my mind in fear. I would pray, recite Bible verses, or sing songs in a frantic attempt to maintain sanity. But my condition worsened until I was nearly unable to care for myself. There were dreadful moments when I feared that I might lose all control and actually take my own life.

Guilt and confusion haunted me night and day. Guilt, because my intense self-preoccupation left no room for the inmates I longed to help. And confusion, because I couldn't understand why I felt this way. I had lost all confidence that my work could ever make a difference in the lives of inmates. It all seemed so hopeless.

Disillusionment gave way to bitterness. Bitterness spawned anger, and the anger compounded my despair. I felt like someone in mourning. I was grieving over the loss of idealism and my failure to change the prison system. Even though I had given it everything, I felt that I couldn't change what I had set out to change. I had failed the inmates and myself.

HELPING OTHERS WITHOUT CRIPPLING YOURSELF

I did recover. It took nearly three years of rest, counseling, meditation, proper nutrition, exercise, and what seemed like infinite patience. But with recovery came a greater awareness of what it means to help others without crippling yourself.

What caused this nightmare? How could I experience such bad feelings when I was only trying to help others? While the experience was overwhelming and confusing at the time, the reasons are fairly simple. Although this happened to me while it was my full-time job to help others, I believe that it provides lessons for anyone involved in helping relationships.

LESSON 1: IT'S ALL ABOUT PEOPLE

When I first began my work in prisons, I was focused on helping individual prisoners. Had you asked me early on about my work, I would have told you about Harold, Sam, Esther, Martina, or Slick. I wanted to give them the tools they needed to grow as human beings and make responsible decisions. More than a few times prisoners or their family members told me the program saved their lives.

Somehow my focus changed. I became less concerned with the person in prison and more concerned with the prison system itself. I was no longer satisfied to help one person at a time. I needed to change an entire penal system—a system that in my view maimed human beings under the guise of rehabilitation. That cause consumed me, leaving all else in its wake.

The key to any successful volunteer opportunity is keeping it focused on a person. Avoid the temptation to transfer your commitment to a problem at the expense of the person you are helping. You can make a difference in a person's life, whereas a major social ill—whether AIDS, drug abuse, or illiteracy—can overwhelm you.

My disillusionment was due in large part to my focus shift: from the individual to the system. How could my impact on a massive institution be measured? When my focus was on prisoners, I knew that I was making a difference.

Am I suggesting that you should never get involved in eradicating a social ill or supporting a noble cause like prison reform? Not at all. But I am suggesting that social, political, and environmental activism must never be conducted at the expense of keeping people in focus. Instead, the activism must proceed hand in hand with a careful concern for and interaction with the people who are faced with the problem.

Jessica Mitford documented the myth of rehabilitation in her book, *Kind and Usual Punishment*. Faced with the evidence, she asked an inmate whether the prison system should be abolished or reformed. He wasn't sure, but he responded, "If I've got cancer, don't wait for the definitive cure to be discovered before treating me."[1]

Bob Ainsworth, former Vice President of World Vision, an international relief organization, demonstrated the power of this personal focus. On a trip to Africa with relief workers and donors, Bob's behavior stood in sharp contrast with the others. While they were offended and overwhelmed by the sights, sounds, and smells of abject poverty, Bob got down on his knees in the street to share magic tricks and treats with the delighted children. No, that wasn't the answer to their plight. But Bob was able to function in a terrible situation because he never lost sight of the children.

LESSON 2: UNDERSTAND YOUR MOTIVES

Somewhere between helping other people and burnout, my motives changed. My early work with prisoners was the most exhilarating experience of my life. Seven inmates and I built a paperback library for nearly five hundred prisoners. When they first asked for my help, I declined for a very good reason: I didn't know the first thing about setting up a library of any kind, especially not a prison library. How could we set up a library for five hundred men on a budget of one hundred dollars per month? The prisoners challenged me: "Let's figure it out together!" We did. The project succeeded because the inmates had a strong desire for reading materials. I wanted to help them.

The Attica project was different from the very beginning. It was my opportunity to establish the largest college education program in the worst prison in the country. I wanted that achievement. Helping the inmates was always part of the process, but at a deeper level, my purpose was to set up a program that would make a mark. It was my program.

There is nothing wrong with the desire to succeed. But when the drive for success overshadows the concern to help others, we are not simply helping other people; we are using them to attain our true goal, success. It violates the spirit of volunteerism. This is not an easy distinction to make because it is a matter of our inner motivation, a matter of the heart. But the people we help will be able to tell whether our heart is set on helping them or achieving something for ourselves through helping them. When our ultimate goal is achievement, the people we help feel used. And we become used up—burned out—in the process.

Helping others can become a thinly veiled attempt to win the approval of those we help because we're starving for approval. Volunteerism, especially person-to-person, can provide a great deal of affirmation for the one doing the helping. When the affirmation becomes the goal rather than the wonderful times that hunger for approval is never satisfied. Sometimes it places a subtle pressure on the person helped to meet our own need for acceptance.

LESSON 3: COUNT THE COST
OF THE VOLUNTEER SITUATION

Prisons are not friendly places. By design, a prison is not a nice place to live in—or to visit. Prison is a place where people are sent as punishment. It seldom disappoints.

One concern drives the penal setting: security. Everything from meals to personal hygiene defers to the demands of security. My work in prisons was often subverted by this institutional preoccupation with security. Papers from our office were destroyed in a search for contraband. Staff members were subjected to body searches. A policy could be implemented or rescinded without question for security reasons.

Working in a hostile environment like a prison takes something out of you. There's a cost involved, a price to be paid. The amount of energy required to function in a setting like that probably varies from person to person. For some people the cost is too high. It simply takes too much energy.

Because it's a hidden cost and more difficult to measure, the cost of working in a hostile environment is easy to underestimate. I allowed myself to get in over my head at Attica, because I failed to count the cost of working in such a hostile context.

When you are counting the cost of a particular volunteer opportunity, remember to include the cost of working in a stressful environment. Some—not all!—options to help take place in high stress environments. Simply functioning in those settings takes something out of you. And the cost varies from person to person. If you are an introvert, it will take more out of you to function in a setting that requires interaction with a lot of other people. If you are an extrovert, you may actually be energized by the experience.

LESSON 4: KNOW WHEN TO SAY WHEN

When I left my job at Attica, six people were doing what I had done alone for months. A reasonable person would have resigned before being incapacitated. But people obsessed with helping ignore reason and seldom admit to being in over their heads.

Why didn't I get out sooner? First of all, I felt I could not "betray" the inmates. A hundred and fifty maximum security prisoners were counting on me. Can you see what I was suffering from? A messiah complex. If I didn't do something, nobody would. I was the answer to their problems. I took on my own shoulders an exaggerated sense of responsibility.

Later, I discovered a deeper reason preventing me from calling it quits sooner. I was afraid of failure—failing the inmates, failing myself. I was literally willing to face personal ruin rather than accept the fact that I couldn't accomplish my goal. I've since learned that the fear of failure is a taskmaster I don't want to serve.

What are the indications that enough is enough? When is time to say when? Consider the following signs:

- Do you approach the volunteer experience with an ongoing sense of dread? (Something beyond the initial nervousness that fades with experience.)
- Do you feel overwhelmed?
- Is the person you are helping retreating from you, despite your continued efforts to make a connection?
- Is the person you are helping antagonistic or threatening toward you?
- Are you afraid?
- Do you feel that you need to spend an inordinate amount of time recovering from your volunteer experience, that is, something more than the usual need to wind down after stimulating activity?

If you answer yes to any of these questions, it's time to evaluate your volunteer experience. Is it really workable? Are there adjustments that can be made to improve the situation? Is it time to say when?

Contact your volunteer coordinator or other responsible person. If your concern cannot be addressed, ask for a different volunteer opportunity. If your concern is not taken seriously, or there is no other option presented, look for a more responsive bridge organization.

LESSON 5: HAVE SOME FUN!

A successful investor once advised me to consider the following question when evaluating my work: "Are you having any fun?" Obviously, this is not the only or the primary criterion. Meaningful activities are not always fun. But it would have been a good question for me to ask before burning out because I was not having fun at Attica. It started out as fun, but it turned into a heavy burden.

Unless we are gaining some measure of satisfaction or enjoyment out of our volunteer relationships, they will come to mean little to us and less to the people we hope to help. Duty is a fine motive for the tasks we cannot avoid—mowing the lawn, paying our bills, flossing our teeth—but it provides inadequate motivation for a relationship with a person with whom we are hoping to share friendship and mutual respect. A sense of obligation helps to steady us through times of fluctuating feelings; but if it's our only fuel, we'll end up exhausted.

Guilt is also a dubious motive for helping others. It may get you started, but it doesn't have the power to sustain you. Count on it: the person you help will sense your lack of joy.

Remember, joy is at the heart of God's love toward us. Joy motivates him. He created the universe because he wanted to. Is it any wonder that joy brings life to volunteer relationships? Joy is what touches the lives of the people you seek to help.

How's this for fun? Hosting a birthday party for a class of children in the Head Start program. Or spending your lunch hour once a week with a child who needs a friend. There are so many opportunities to have the time of your life by giving a little bit of yourself to someone in need.

LESSON 6: GET A LIFE!

I experienced burnout when I allowed my work to become an obsession. I sacrificed virtually every dimension of a well-balanced life on the altar of my obsession. I shudder even now as I recall the offering on that altar: friends, proper nutrition, sleep, exercise, social activities. My work became my life. In the end, that strategy served neither the interests of the inmates or myself.

Volunteering is more like a long-distance run than a short sprint. So learn to pace yourself. It's part of your life, to be kept in balance with the other parts.

LESSON 7: GIVE IT ANOTHER DAY

The Attica experience did not work for me and I finally had to resign my position. There may be volunteer opportunities that won't work for you. It doesn't really matter if a volunteer assignment is right for someone else. The situation must be right for you and for the person you help. What does matter, however, is that a failure doesn't take you out of the game. Try again. Don't let one unhappy experience deter you from experiencing the joy of helping someone else. I'm glad I didn't.

Subsequent opportunities are often more rewarding than initial experiences. We have tested the water, experimented with our strokes, and learned valuable lessons about ourselves and others in the process. We have a far better idea of what we can do.

Rose had a devastating experience volunteering at her church. She had given countless hours to the children in the Sunday school program. Her most recent role was supervisory, but Rose wanted to return to teaching a class. She thrived on that firsthand experience. But the new superintendent had other ideas. As improbable as it sounds, he actually refused to give this veteran teacher, loved by children and parents alike, a class. If she wouldn't serve where the system needed her most, he felt, she wouldn't serve at all.

Rose was shattered. An experienced teacher rejected. Does it get any worse than this? But Rose's frustration with the Sunday school didn't change her love for children. She preferred to work with children in the church setting, but since that door was closed, she walked through another one.

Rose volunteered to care for the children of disadvantaged parents involved in a class on managing finances. This new experience introduced Rose to the enormous needs of children from families in poverty. She now believes that God worked through a difficult situation to lead her to this new opportunity. Rather than giving up in a huff, Rose has gotten to know kids like Alice, John, Jacob, Cara, Katie, and Andrew—kids on the other side of a new opportunity.

LESSON 9: IT DOESN'T ALL DEPEND ON ME

People who suffer from a messiah complex have not learned how to accurately measure their contributions. They tend to view the part they play as irreplaceable instead of merely important. Some of our contributions in life are irreplaceable. For example, I am—at least in some sense—irreplaceable as a father to my children. But those contributions are the exception, not the norm.

In most arenas, my contributions are important—perhaps vitally important—but not irreplaceable. Part of my recovery from caring too much—or more accurately, caring without proper perspective—came when I learned that it doesn't all depend on me.

A lengthy trip with major commitments was almost over. I sat at the airport gate feeling exhausted. Then I saw him. An elderly man sitting in a wheelchair, crying. I heard him tell someone that he had just buried his wife.

I felt that I should provide some comfort to the man in his time of grief. But my strength was gone, including my emotional reserves. So I just sat there, feeling guilty. Moments later, an airline employee sat next to the man and listened to his pain. Then it was time to board the plane. I was looking forward to avoiding the man's grief and my guilt over not responding. But it wasn't to be. The man took his seat in the row ahead of me. He continued to sob.

Two conflicting voices waged a war inside my heart. The first urged immediate action, threatening swift condemnation if I neglected to help this poor soul. The other voice whispered caution. I wasn't the only possible answer to this man's pain.

Before long, a Catholic nun took her seat next to the older gentleman. This was her assignment, not mine. The lesson for me was clear: I have limits and there are others who care. It doesn't all depend on me. In the drama of life, I'm not the playwright, director, stage manager, and leading character rolled into one. I only play a part, assigned by the One who can draw upon an infinite storehouse of riches.

ELEVEN

Pioneering a Dream

A N ADVENTUROUS BATTALION COMMANDER in the Roman army once led his soldiers beyond the borders known to the mapmakers. Keep in mind that during the time of the Roman Empire, mapmaking was a primitive science at best. These early cartographers drew what was known on their maps, filling in the remaining area with symbols of dragons, monsters, and big fish. When the commander looked at his map, he could see that he was in the territory represented by dragons and monsters. He didn't want to turn around and go back, but neither did he want to pursue his course without further instruction. So he dispatched a messenger to Rome with this urgent request: "Please send new orders. We have marched off the map!"[1]

In many respects, the new volunteers are a grass roots movement of pioneers. The massive social needs of our cities, schools, and families, are similar to the unconquered American West of the nineteenth century. And within the larger movement of volunteers, some will march into uncharted territory, discovering new ways of helping people.

We know that the bureaucratic approach of government cannot replace the power of individuals, churches, and groups of volunteers to help people in need. The system is not the solution, but people helping others, person by person and person *to* person. What the politicians call the "private sector" is waking up. We're beginning to launch bold new initiatives into the unmapped realms of human need. People are starting to emphasize again the importance of helping a neighbor in need.

WANTED: DREAMERS AND PIONEERS

In an age of discovery, we need dreamers. We need people who can see new possibilities beyond the known and the established and the already organized. But more than dreamers, we need pioneers. We need people whose dreams are not merely flights of fancy but people who wrestle with their dreams until they find one that breaks into reality.

The business of people helping people is a dreamer's market. There is a vast territory of human need which is unexplored. New initiatives are being born every day.

Millard Fuller had a dream: to bring people together to build homes for the poor. His dream was eventually realized when *Habitat for Humanity*—well known for the involvement of former President Jimmy Carter—was born.

Michael Friedline had a dream: to link members of a local church with one homeless family to help them break the cycle of poverty. Out of this dream Project Home Again came into being.

The mother of a child killed by a drunk driver was living through a nightmare of grief. In the midst of her pain, she had a dream: to organize other moms to fight drunk driving. She pioneered MADD, Mothers Against Drunk Driving, which has become one of the most effective voices in the campaign to eradicate this menace.

Pioneers come in all shapes and sizes. Many of the best and brightest dreams are never replicated beyond the neighborhood or community they serve. They may never gain national recognition or require a name, a trademark, or incorporation papers. They may involve only a few people.

Two women from a Catholic parish in Seattle began a ministry to infants born into poverty even though few people realized there was such a need. Their first client was a young mother who arrived at a local shelter with a three-year-old child and her newborn infant with placenta and umbilical cord attached. The baby didn't even have a blanket.

These pioneers secured a tooth-marked crib as a collection box. It was placed in the sanctuary near the communion railing. Within fourteen months, they received and distributed over 60 thousand dollars worth of basic goods to moms and newborns. Local businesses and high school students are pitching in.

Alice saw a need to provide baby cribs for poor families in Denver. She began to shop for cribs at garage sales and discovered that these sales were also an excellent source for children's clothing. But that was just the beginning. Alice found that she could teach disadvantaged moms how to shop the garage sales and stretch their money. She also found a local church willing to donate space to store the cribs.

A group of pilots wanted to put their flying skills to use for people in need. They formed a nonprofit corporation for the purpose of flying people with severe medical problems to specialty clinics around the country. Every patient flown has a verified medical and financial need.

A newly widowed woman launched the *New to You* Store to provide used clothing for the poor. The store meets the needs of many disadvantaged customers and in the process provides several widows with an opportunity to gather to talk, sew, sort clothes, and pray.

A member of Calvary Church was concerned about the growing number of latchkey kids in town—children who return to an empty home because their parents are working and unable to afford child care. The church launched an after-school ministry where volunteers work with kids who come to the church facility from school until their parents return from work.

John Gardner, the former Secretary of Health, Education, and Welfare, observed in the foreword of the book, *America's Voluntary Spirit*, that "virtually every significant social idea in this country has been nurtured in the private sector."[2] That's us! These "significant social ideas" were pioneered by individuals, working together with others who shared their dream, to launch a creative new approach to helping people in need.

I HAD A DREAM

In 1976, I was the director of a social service organization with a shrinking resource base. There were more people than ever to help with less money. As a lifelong churchgoer, I was also aware that few individuals that I met in church were active in helping needy people on a one to one basis. I felt like someone standing between these two vast groups of people: those in dire need on the one hand and those with a philosophy to help, but little opportunity, on the other. Out of sheer frustration more than any creative impulse, the obvious thought occurred to me: Why not build a bridge between these two groups?

First, I had to test the hypothesis that the people involved in church activities were not taking a more active concern for the poor for lack of meaningful opportunity. So I asked them, "When was the last time you had an opportunity to help a poor person directly, not just through contributing to a charity or paying taxes?" Not much of a response. Many could only think of a church-sponsored food drive or the yearly project to distribute Christmas baskets to needy families.

Why not transform the social service agency that I worked for into a bridge between people in churches who wanted to help and people who needed their help? The agency would provide no direct services to the poor. It would only provide the crucial link between the poor and those individuals who were willing to help them. (Our new motto—"We will not knowingly help anyone"—was not a stroke of fundraising genius!)

I relied on colleagues within the helping agencies and churches to provide reality checks on the evolving idea. They helped me shape the idea and suggested the name for it. The small group of trusted people were my support group when other people were telling me that such a simple idea could never work. The agency people doubted that churches would respond. The pastors were cynical about the willingness of agencies to work cooperatively with them. Fortunately, both were wrong.

There were times when the criticism, combined with the enormity of the task, nearly defeated the dream. Some nights I woke up in a cold sweat. But I persisted. Whenever possible I tried to learn from the criticism. I asked the critics to be as specific as possible about their misgivings. I confess now, with some reluctance, that the honest criticism was more valuable to the dream than some of the applause.

Eventually, seventy-eight churches in my home town agreed to participate in the first expression of what became LOVE INC—the bridge between people in need and congregations who wanted to help. In the first year the social service agency, redesigned to become a bridge, was able to witness more needs met than the previous year. Yet our budget decreased. LOVE INC programs are now active in ninety-two communities and have mobilized over one hundred thousand volunteers in the four countries. It is literally a dream coming true.

ALLOW TIME FOR YOUR DREAM TO HATCH

Dreams take time to develop. A dream may begin as a nebulous longing to do something for a particular group of people. You begin to imagine different ways of tackling a pressing problem. In embryo form, a dream may be nothing more than a flight of fancy. But then your imagination is captivated by a particular way to help people. Your dream is taking shape.

Be sure to give your dream time to incubate. Over time,

your imaginings will gain substance. You will begin to mentally test your developing idea. As you compare your dream with reality, your dream will be adjusted.

You probably aren't ready to put a dream into practice until you can put it into words—a vision statement, one or two simple sentences that capture the essence of your idea. I have an African-American friend who has always dreamed of providing some help to those who share his heritage. The other day, he said to me, "I've been thinking of starting a support group for young men who have fathered children out of wedlock, something to help them take some responsibility for their children." He was making a concise vision statement. He was not expressing a vague longing to help people. He was putting his dream into words—a specific way to help people with specific needs.

RUB SHOULDERS AND SHAPE A DREAM

Now that my friend has put words to his dream he can rub shoulders with young men who have fathered children out of wedlock or share his idea with those who have close contact with them—all the while allowing his dream to be tested and shaped by the interaction. How could he get in touch with these young men? Would a group setting be an effective way of reaching them? What would motivate young men in this position to be interested in this kind of help? What kind of investment of time and energy would it take?

Helpful ideas for serving people are seldom found in isolation from the people to be served or those who are working closely with them. So before you launch a brand new organization to realize your dream, begin to rub shoulders with the group of people you want to help. If you have a creative idea about how to help the homeless, your first step is to get to know some homeless people and those who are already helping them.

You may feel that the traditional soup kitchen isn't a very

effective way to provide food for homeless people. You have a better idea. But have you ever spent time with homeless people? Maybe you should begin by helping out at one of those soup kitchens so you can meet some homeless people. As you rub shoulders with real people in need, you will be able to test your idea. Without realizing it, the people you intend to help will become your partners in shaping your idea to fit reality.

Most ideas for new ways to help people must undergo significant adjustments as they interact with reality. A dream is a picture of what might be, not a blueprint to follow regardless of the facts. People who are so attached to the specific details of their dreams do not become pioneers; they become frustrated dreamers.

GREAT IDEAS NEED PATIENT DREAMERS

Some ideas flop because they just don't square with reality. But the lack of early results doesn't always mean you have a bad idea. It may simply be a matter of timing. A recovering alcoholic named Steve found immense benefit from the Twelve Steps of Recovery advocated by Alcoholics Anonymous. There was no AA meeting in Steve's town and he knew there was a great need. So Steve started his own AA meeting. He arranged to use the local Red Cross building, advertised the meeting, arrived early to get the coffee going—and waited. Nobody came. He repeated the same ritual next week with the same result.

Steve was the only participant in the AA meeting on Tuesday nights for five months before the first person showed up. But Steve was patient. For him this wasn't an experiment in helping people. He knew there was a desperate need in his town, and he knew that an AA meeting would help. Besides, he desperately needed the support that a meeting would bring.

Today, there are at least three meetings of Alcoholics Anonymous each day of the week. Steve has never received an award or any other public recognition. He has never been paid for his services. But Steve's persistence has paid great dividends —for himself and for many other recovering alcoholics.[3]

EVERY DREAM HAS TO RUN THE GAUNTLET

Virtually every new idea will be challenged by those who claim it can't be done. There's no avoiding this process. If you simply keep the idea to yourself and launch it without sharing it with others you will lose the advantage of constructive criticism. And you will be very much on your own. On the other hand, if you share your dream with others, you will invite a litany of reasons why your idea could never happen.

Some people are constitutionally cautious. They are the naysayers and every new idea will attract their comments. I have heard these comments for much of my life and have developed my own responses:

COMMENT: If that were such a good idea, someone would have tried it long ago.

REPLY: If everyone thought like that, there would be no new ideas.

COMMENT: Nothing that simple can work.

REPLY: That's what they said about the wheel too.

COMMENT: What gives you the idea that you can figure out that problem when no one else can? Better brains than you have tried and failed.

REPLY: Never underestimate the power of God, even to use someone like me.

We don't need to cave in to the pessimism of the naysayers. But we shouldn't despise them either. They provide a service. They challenge you to think, to ask questions, to tackle problems—and if nothing else, to test your own resolve.

Anyone with a new idea must learn how to sift genuinely constructive criticism from the criticism of pessimism. What is behind a person's advice? Is he or she speaking from experience or simply critiquing from a distance? Does the advisor have any empathy with your passion? Give greater weight to warmhearted advice. Is the adviser offering stock advice where you get the feeling that any new idea would elicit the same response, or is it backed up by wise insight? Listen carefully; you will be able to tell the difference.

DO YOUR HOMEWORK

In order to put shoes on your dream, you have to do some homework.

1. Is my dream a realistic response to an actual need? A congregation in one town decided to provide hot lunches for the homeless in July. After promotion, planning, and preparation, no one showed up for the lunches. If they had held the hot lunch in the dead of winter, the response might well have been more encouraging. Their idea hadn't passed the reality test.

I discovered evidence for a need in one community quite by accident. I was being interviewed on a radio talk show about how churches can develop ways to help people in need. In the course of the interview, I mentioned a hypothetical project: "For example, a church in this town might develop an inexpensive Mom's Time Out program. Moms could drop their kids off at the church for two to three hours on specific days." During the call-in segment of the interview, a young mother called. She got right to the point: "Where is the church with the Mom's Time Out program?" My offhand comment had touched on a real need.

2. Put your dream into words: a vision statement. A vision statement must be specific and concise. If it takes you ten minutes to describe what you have in mind, you probably need to focus on the heart of the matter. Remember the vision statement of Federal Express, one of the most successful delivery services: "Overnight."

Putting a man on the moon was an incredibly complex task, but it was possible to state the vision in a simple sentence: we intend to land a manned spacecraft on the moon and return. If you can't make a simple and concise statement right away, continue to do other aspects of your homework until you can.

3. What are my expectations for the people who will benefit from this idea? Will this project relieve need through the provision of goods and services? Is this project designed to help people move from dependence to greater independence? Must those who benefit be highly motivated to participate? How will I know when I have succeeded?

4. Is the help I envision already available? Are those services adequate? In my hometown, there are several places homeless people can go for free clothing. In fact, clothing is so readily available that those who use it simply throw it away and acquire some more. It's cheaper than cleaning the dirty stuff. If someone came to me with an idea to provide clothing for the homeless, I would suggest they look into a way to provide laundry facilities instead.

5. How do I get in touch with the people I would like to help? This is one of the major challenges new ideas must wrestle with. Having received several requests for a telephone reassurance program linking elderly shut-ins with volunteers who could call them on a regular basis, I was fairly convinced of the need. I tried three times to launch just such a program, but each time it has failed. Each time, I could find the callers, but not the people in need of a regular phone call. The need is still there, but so far I don't know how to reach the people in need.

SMALL IS BEAUTIFUL

Many dreamers naturally think in large-scale terms. But most successful ventures begin as small projects. A healthy plant depends on a viable seed. So pay careful attention to the seed.

Before you advertise to care for the masses, begin to work with a small group of needy individuals. Don't promise the moon. Keep it simple. Avoid hype. Make a modest contribution to begin with.

Before you try to mobilize an army of volunteers, try it yourself—if the essential task can be done by one person. Then work together with a few interested individuals. This small beginning will allow you to be flexible in your approach so that you can learn as you go.

NEVER FORGET THE POWER OF ONE

Remember, one person is worth helping. After all, isn't that the vision that got you started in the first place—the possibility of actually making a difference for another human being? If that isn't worthwhile, then what is the sense in volunteering? If you cook up a program that grows but loses a vision of the individual person helped, what have you gained? First learn how to make it personal and make it bigger only as you are able to find ways to keep it personal.

Government agencies think in terms of "number of clients served" and "units distributed." But how can you measure the value of one person who is helped by another? The fact is, it can't be measured and that's why it's a treasure never to lose sight of. So while you're dreaming big dreams, don't forget to think small. Don't lose sight of the power and the value of one person helping another person.

TWELVE

Quiet Heroes

OUR AGE IS STARVED FOR HEROES. Not just figures from the past or the celebrities of contemporary culture, but real heroes. People whose deeds inspire.

I know people all over this country who are heroes. When I'm feeling cynical about the latest scandal in high places, they remind me of the dignity of being human. If you're looking for people like this, I can tell you where to find some. Don't look in the newspapers or on television; most of their biographies will never be written. Just look wherever people need helping—among the victims of crushing disease, the terminally ill, the elderly, the homeless and the hungry, the addicted, the physically and mentally handicapped, disadvantaged students struggling to stay in school, the children of poverty and the parents and grandparents trying to raise them.

When you begin to help other people through volunteering, you will begin to discover a new breed of quiet heroes. You will meet ordinary people who make you proud to be a human being again. You will discover people like Angela.

ANGELA'S STORY

Angela had two children of her own when she was a child of fifteen. She lied about her age to get a job. When she was found out, she lost the job and landed on the welfare rolls.

A few years later the owner of Angela's building abandoned it. The same thing was happening to a lot of buildings in her largely Latino neighborhood. The buildings were eventually condemned and the tenants evicted.

Eventually, Angela was the only tenant in her building left with no place to go. On welfare with two children and a sixth-grade education, she didn't have much of a future either. She kept alive through the winter by keeping all the stove burners on. It wasn't very safe, but it beat the cold.

Then a small group of volunteers began working with the tenants in the abandoned building across the street. They were trying to help keep those families from being displaced by repairing anything that might get the building condemned—one apartment at a time.

Every time Angela saw the leader of the volunteers walking across the street, she hid, turned out the lights, and kept the kids quiet. She had been told that he was buying up all the property and evicting the tenants. Besides he was an Anglo, and Angela wasn't inclined to trust him.

When Angela later found out the man was a minister, she wasn't reassured. Angela's great grandmother had told her that she could always count on the church to help her in times of need. But that wasn't the way Angela saw things. She heard from her great grandmother about a Jesus who took care of the sick and helped the poor; but when she went to church for help, she was told that the church wasn't in the welfare business.

Fortunately, Jim didn't live up to her expectations. The volunteers—mainly white, middle-class, college students off for the summer—set to work on her building. Out of sheer curiosity Angela came to their opening chapel service, held in the building. The text for Jim's sermon was from the words of Jesus, "As you do to the least of these my brothers, you do it unto me." It reminded her of the Jesus her great grandmother used to talk about.

"FREE WORK? NO WAY!"

Angela's building, brought back from the brink of being condemned, was becoming a beacon in her neighborhood. The volunteers opened a health clinic. One of the physicians asked Angela if she would be interested in volunteering at the clinic. Her first response was, "Free work? No way!" But eventually she began to answer the clinic telephone a few hours each day.

As a volunteer, Angela began to change her way of thinking about welfare. "For a long time, I felt that the government owed me this welfare check every month," she explained. "If I didn't get it, boy, I would be on that telephone bawling out my social worker. But I knew that it was time to get honest. 'Nobody owes you anything,' I told myself. 'You owe it to yourself and to your kids to be the best you can be.' I didn't want my daughter to say, 'I want to be just like my mother on welfare: surviving, struggling....'"

"Finally," as Angela tells the story, "I put it all together and said to myself, 'Let's look at what you're doing. You get a welfare check every month. Think about it as a scholarship, just like you're in college.' So I did. The building became my college. I was living on campus in my downstairs apartment. The Health Services Clinic was my classroom. I was getting scholarship money—my welfare check—to go to school. Like anyone else on a scholarship, I was being paid to learn."

Angela began to learn with a vengeance. She started out as a volunteer receptionist at the clinic. Then she learned how to balance the clinic checking account. Eventually, she was handling all the bookkeeping for the clinic—and loving it.

Next, she learned how to measure blood pressure, weigh patients, take temperatures, do blood sugars tests—all the skills of a medical technician. In time, Angela became so valuable to the clinic that she was offered a staff position. That was the end of welfare, and the beginning of a new life.

Through Angela's quiet example and personal encouragement other women in her neighborhood adopted her new way of thinking about welfare. "That's your scholarship from the government," she told her friends. "While you're on scholarship you better get yourself educated so you can get a real job." Angela encouraged one of her friends, who wanted to work at a pharmacy but didn't have the necessary skills, to volunteer her services for six months. The young woman became so valuable after a few weeks that she was hired at a salary that beat her welfare check.

In addition to her full-time job, Angela still volunteers. She looks at each volunteer opportunity as a part of her continuing education program. Angela has learned the secret of helping others: helping you is helping me.

It may seem as though Angela picked herself up by her own bootstraps and broke the cycle of dependency that is all too often bred by our welfare system. But her story of recovery didn't begin until she met some people who were volunteering their time to fix up an old apartment building.

Those volunteers didn't have to be middle-class college students off for the summer. They might have been blue-collar workers, giving some of their time on weekends, or middle-aged home owners using skills gained from years of fixing their own homes to help those less fortunate. Or they might have been people just like you. Like Angela, they are quiet heroes too. Their efforts to lend a hand to people in need began a chain reaction that produced, in economic terms, a yield totally out of proportion to the original investment. That's how the economy of volunteering works.

VOLUNTEER! YOU MEET THE NICEST PEOPLE

Ron is a friend of mine who took his best shot at doing a good deed. On his way home from the office, a man who looked down and out asked him for some money to buy food. Ron didn't mean to catch the man's attention, but it happened anyway and now he felt a little stuck. He wanted to help, but he didn't know how.

In a moment of what Ron hoped was inspiration—it wasn't —he told the man who was looking for a handout: "I could give you a few dollars, but that wouldn't get you very far in the little corner stores around here. Tell you what—I'll pick up some groceries for you on my way home. I'll meet you back at this intersection tomorrow morning at 8:30 with the groceries."

Ron went home feeling great. He picked up two full bags of groceries—good, nutritious food. He was happy to know that his handout was going to something worthwhile and wasn't being used to purchase drugs or alcohol. On his way back to work the next morning, he was feeling even better—that "helpers high" I told him about was kicking in.

No, the man who asked him for the handout didn't show up at the prearranged time and place. Ron stood there in his business suit, holding his briefcase and two bags of groceries for longer than he'd like to admit. When the office secretary asked him what the groceries were for, he sighed and said, "Long story...."

Ron's intentions were good, and he gets an A for effort, but he was missing something: experience helping people in need. If Ron had volunteered his time through a good bridge organization, he might have met someone who knows the score a little better than he did. He might have met someone like Angela. Someone who could help him put his time and money to much better use.

Perhaps you can identify with Ron. You recognize the need, and you want to lend a hand, but you're not sure where to begin. Perhaps you are like the man on the plane who wanted to help young people in south Los Angeles or any other major city. By connecting with a good bridge organization you might meet another quiet hero named Karen.

"WHO'S YOUR MOTHER?"

Karen grew up in a neighborhood infested with drugs. Like Angela, her life was touched by the help of some volunteers.

She began to help others and in the process helped herself.

As a mother of four, Karen's heart was broken at the sight of young teenage boys selling drugs on one street corner. Karen went up to one of the boys selling drugs and asked, "Who is your mother?"

"Why would you want to know?" he asked.

"I just asked who your mother is—you're not ashamed of your mother are you?" Karen replied.

Before too long, Karen had the names of several mothers. Over the next few days, she paid each one a call. Some knew their sons were dealing drugs, some didn't. But all were concerned and didn't know what to do. Karen didn't know what to do either, but she invited the mothers of those youngsters to come with her to the corner where their sons were selling.

That first evening, the group of moms stood on the other side of the street watching their sons. Their mere presence put a crimp in the drug trade that night. Later they began to pass out flyers to the people coming down to buy the drugs. The flyers informed potential buyers that the young men selling the drugs were their sons: would they take their business elsewhere?

Some of the mothers followed their sons into the alleys when they tried to make a transaction. They didn't berate them, but they sure didn't show any signs of approval either.

Those moms had quite an effect on the boys. With their mothers around, they lost all interest in selling drugs. Led by Karen, the mothers got their sons together and began to talk about alternatives to selling drugs. The boys wanted out, but they didn't feel they could do it alone. They needed help.

The next day Karen and the group of mothers took the boys across the street to one of their homes. Karen got the ball rolling with a question. "We want to find out: if you could be anything in this God-given world, what would it be? That's all we want to know." The boys started to talk, and the mothers started writing it all down.

Karen and the other moms arranged for the boys to work with mentors who would teach them a trade in exchange for some volunteer work. One boy wanted to be a barber. So they found a barber willing to show him his trade in exchange for some help cleaning up from the young man on Saturdays.

Karen also started a support group for the boys. At the meetings, she talked to them about babies who were addicted to drugs through their pregnant mothers. They took a field trip to the local hospital to see the effect of the drugs on those innocent victims.

One of the boys came to Karen saying, "Teach me to read. If you teach me how to read, I'll be all right." So Karen began to look for people who could work one-on-one with the young men who couldn't read. Karen, who served as a community volunteer, became a contact point between those teenagers who wanted to find a way out of the drug culture and other volunteers.

Chances are you could never do what Karen did—gain the attention and interest of those mothers and their sons and impart motivation for change. But if Karen knew that you were willing to become a mentor to one of those kids who wanted to learn a trade or teach one of those young men to read, you could begin the adventure of making a difference.

ONE PERSON CAN MAKE A WORLD OF DIFFERENCE

If you told Karen she was a hero, she would laugh in your face. You see, Karen's world is filled with heroes. They are the new volunteers, people lending a hand and making a difference.

Perhaps you are not an inner-city resident who is familiar with the mysterious world of welfare and drugs. You may not be streetwise like Karen. You don't have to be to make a difference. All you have to do is link arms with people like Karen, and together you can get the job done.

There are people like Karen and her friends all over this country. They aren't waiting for the government to develop new policies to save our cities, clean up the environment, reform our educational and health care systems, and rescue our children. They are rolling up their sleeves and lending a hand to people in need—one person at a time.

Other people may look at the forest, but they look at the individual trees. And they are finding that with some personal attention, those trees can be helped.

Most are ordinary people like you and me and the people we know. They don't think of themselves as heroes. They don't see themselves as martyrs. They feel too good about what they're doing for that. They are discovering something that we never should have lost sight of in the first place: one person lending a hand to another person can make a world of difference. That person could be you. Like so many others, you may find that in the process of helping one other person, at least two people benefit. Try it out and see for yourself: helping you is helping me.

1

Local and State Volunteer Opportunities

THE VOLUNTEER CENTER DIRECTORY is provided through the courtesy of the Points of Light Foundation and is a good resource for investigating local and state volunteer opportunities. For more information about this directory, please call: 1-800-879-5400.

ALASKA
Willie Taylor
Director
Information & Referral Service
United Way of Anchorage
341 West Tudor Road, Suite 106
Anchorage, AK 99503-6638
Phone: (907) 562-4483
Fax: (907) 563-0020

Brenda Holden
Director
Volunteer Action Center
P.O. Box 74396
Fairbanks, AK 99707
Phone: (907) 452-7000
Fax: (907) 452-7270

ALABAMA
State Office:
Pat Thompson
Director

Governor's Office on Volunteerism
11 South Union Street, Room 219
Montgomery, AL 36130
Phone: (205) 242-4511
Fax: (205) 242-4407

Lynn Collins
Director
Volunteer Center of Calhoun County
407 Noble Street
P.O. Box 1122
Anniston, AL 36202
Phone: (205) 236-8229

Mary K. Braddock
Director
Volunteer Center of Morgan County
P.O. Box 986
Decatur, AL 35602-0986
Phone: (205) 355-8628
Fax: (205) 355-8628

Betty P. Hubbard
Director
Volunteer Center of
  Huntsville/Madison County
P.O. Box 18094
1101 Washington Street
Huntsville, AL 35804
Phone: (205) 539-7797
Fax: (205) 539-5914

Susan Wininger
Director
United Way Volunteer Center
3600 8th Avenue South
P.O. Box 320189
Birmingham, AL 35222
Phone: (205) 251-5131
Fax: (205) 323-2872

Linda Yeend
Executive Director
Volunteer Action of
  The Eastern Shore
P.O. Box 61
Fairhope, AL 36532
Phone: (205) 928-0509

Frances M. Dendy
Director
Volunteer Mobile, Inc.
2504 Dauphin Street, Suite K
Mobile, AL 36606
Phone: (205) 479-0631

Doci Haslam
Director
Voluntary Action Center
Information & Referral
P.O. Box 11044
Montgomery, AL 36111-0044
Phone: (205) 284-0006
Fax: (205) 281-9184

ARKANSAS
State Office:
Billie Ann Myers
Director

Arkansas Division of Volunteerism
P.O. Box 1437
Slot 1300
Little Rock, AR 72203
Phone: (501) 682-7540
Fax: (501) 682-6571

Linda Martin
Director
Voluntary Action Center
222 Van Buren
Camden, AR 71701
Phone: (501) 836-8166

Beth Walker
Director
Volunteer Center of United Way of
  Pulaski County
P.O. Box 3257
Little Rock, AR 72203-3257
Phone: (501) 376-4567
Fax: (501) 376-7607

Norma McLain
Pres. of the Board & Director,
  RSVP
Volunteer Center of Hot Springs &
  Garland Counties
P.O. Box 821
Hot Springs, AR 71902
Phone: (501) 623-6830
Fax: (501) 624-2064

Rocio Leach
Coordinator
Volunteer Center of
  Crittendon County
P.O. Box 2990
780 North Airport Road
West Memphis, AR 72303
Phone: (501) 735-4373
Fax: (501) 732-7504

ARIZONA
Marcia Streets
Director
Volunteer Center of Pinal County

P.O. Box 10541
1201 North Pinal Avenue, Suite A
Casa Grande, AZ 85222
Phone: (602) 836-0736
Fax: (602) 836-0737

Lucie Causey
Director
Volunteer Center of
    Maricopa County
1515 East Osborn
Phoenix, AZ 85014
Phone: (602) 263-9736
Fax: (602) 631-4865

Sandra Wagner
Director
Volunteer Center of Yavapai County
107 North Cortez, Room 303
Prescott, AZ 86301
Phone: (602) 776-9908

Ellen Hargis
Executive Director
Volunteer Center
877 South Alvernon Way
Tucson, AZ 85711
Phone: (602) 327-6207
Fax: (602) 795-8948

CALIFORNIA
Richard Yanes
Director
Volunteer Center of Placer County
DeWitt Center
11566 D Avenue
Auburn, CA 95603
Phone: (916) 885-7706

Tish Sammon
Director
Volunteer Center of
    El Dorado County
3430 Robin Lane, Building 2
Cameron Park, CA 95682
Phone: (916) 676-8353
Fax: (916) 676-8356

Peggy White
Director
Volunteer Center of Contra Costa
1070 Concord Avenue, Suite 100
Concord, CA 94520
Phone: (510) 246-1050
Fax: (510) 246-1064

Reba Kickliter
Director
Volunteer Center of Kern County, Inc.
601 Chester Avenue
Bakersfield, CA 93301
Phone: (805) 327-9346

Janet R. Summerville
Director
Community Action Volunteers in
    Education (CAVE)
West 2nd & Cherry Streets
Chico, CA 95929-0750
Phone: (916) 895-5817

Lynda Nield
Director
Volunteer Center, City of Davis
23 Russell Blvd.
Davis, CA 95616
Phone: (916) 757-5626

Norma L. Coffey
Director
Downey Volunteer Center
11026 Downey Avenue
Downey, CA 90241
Phone: (310) 861-1712

Gail R. Doswell
Director (Interim)
Volunteer Center of
    Solano County
744 Empire Street, Suite 204
Fairfield, CA 94533
Phone: (707) 427-6699

Will Wiebe
Director
Volunteer Bureau of Fresno County

1900 Mariposa Mall, Suite 303
Fresno, CA 93721
Phone: (209) 237-3101

Beverly Hayward
Director
Volunteer Action Center of
    Nevada County
10139 Joerschke Drive
Grass Valley, CA 95945
Phone: (916) 272-5041

Lana daSilva
Director
Volunteer Bureau of Kings County
213 West 7th, Suite 6
Hanford, CA 93230
Phone: (209) 582-3455

Debbie Ellis
Executive Director
Volunteer Center
Orange County West
16168 Beach Boulevard, Suite 121
Huntington Beach, CA 92647
Phone: (714) 375-7751
Fax: (714) 375-7757

Tania Rash
Director
La Mirada Volunteer Center
12900 Bluefield Avenue
La Mirada, CA 90638
Phone: (310) 943-0131
Fax: (310) 947-5021

Charles A. Fox
Director
Volunteer Center of Los Angeles
2117 West Temple Street
3rd Floor
Los Angeles, CA 90026
Phone: (213) 484-2849
Fax: (213) 484-8011

Sharon King
Executive Director
Volunteer Center Stanislaus
2937 Veneman Avenue, Suite B-100

Modesto, CA 95356
Phone: (209) 524-1307

Lillias W. Coombs
Director
Monrovia Volunteer Center
119 W. Palm Avenue
Monrovia, CA 91016
Phone: (818) 357-3797

Jane Maines
Director
Volunteer Center of
    Monterey County
801 Lighthouse Avenue
Monterey, CA 93940
Phone: (408) 655-9234
Fax: (408) 655-9244

Christina Cunningham
Director
Volunteer Center of Napa County, Inc.
1820 Jefferson Street
Napa, CA 94559
Phone: (707) 252-6222
Fax: (707) 226-5179

Irene L. Maestri
Director
Volunteer Centers of Alameda
    County, Inc.
1212 Broadway, Suite 622
Oakland, CA 94612
Phone: (415) 893-6239
Fax: (415) 893-5017

Sandy Doerschlog
Director
Volunteer Center of
    San Fernando Valley
8134 Van Nuys Boulevard, #200
Panorama City, CA 91402
Phone: (818) 908-5066
Fax: (818) 908-5147

LeRoy Spargo
Director
Volunteer Center of
    San Gabriel Valley

3301 Thorndale Road
Pasadena, CA 91107
Phone: (818) 792-6118

Sonya Amos
Coordinator
Volunteers Involved for Pasadena
234 East Colorado Boulevard
Room 205
Pasadena, CA 91101
Phone: (818) 796-6926
Fax: (818) 796-5766

Donna Campbell
Executive Director
Valley Volunteer Center
333 Division Street
Pleasanton, CA 94566
Phone: (510) 462-3570
Fax: (510) 462-0596

Ron Alexander
Director
Volunteer Center of
    Greater Pomona Valley
436 West 4th Street, #201
Pomona, CA 91766
Phone: (714) 623-1284
Fax: (714) 623-2568

Grace Slocam
Director
Volunteer Center of Greater Riverside
2060 University Avenue, Suite 212
Riverside, CA 92507
Phone: (714) 686-4402
Fax: (714) 686-7417

Meg Kochendorfer
Director
Voluntary Action of South Lake Tahoe
P.O. Box 878
South Lake Tahoe, CA 96156
Phone: (916) 541-2611
Fax: (916) 541-2611

Margaret Wiemers
Director
Volunteer Center of

Sacramento/Yolo Counties
8912 Volunteer Lane, Suite 140
Sacramento, CA 95826
Phone: (916) 368-3110
Fax: (916) 368-3190

Lenore Jacoby
Director
Volunteer Center of
    The Inland Empire, Inc.
1481 North Waterman, Suite 105
San Bernardino, CA 92404
Phone: (714) 884-2556
Fax: (714) 881-3871

Kelly Lau
Vice President
United Way of San Diego
    Volunteer Center
P.O. Box 23543
San Diego, CA 92193
Phone: (619) 492-2160
Fax: (619) 492-2171

Charles F. Greene
Director
Volunteer Center of San Francisco
1160 Battery Street, Suite 70
San Francisco, CA 94111
Phone: (415) 982-8999
Fax: (415) 399-9214

Siobhan Kenney
Director
Volunteer Exchange of
    Santa Clara County
1922 The Alameda, Suite 211
San Jose, CA 95126
Phone: (408) 286-1126
Fax: (408) 247-5805

Joyce H. Haron
Director
Volunteer Center of San Mateo County
800 South Claremont Suite 108
San Mateo, CA 94402
Phone: (415) 342-0801
Fax: (415) 342-1399

Manuela Arenivas
Director
Volunteer Center—San Pedro
Satellite of Torrance
501 North Mesa
San Pedro, CA 90731
Phone: (310) 519-8955

Tina Cheplick
Director
Volunteer Center of Marin
70 Skyview Terrace
San Rafael, CA 94903
Phone: (415) 479-5660
Fax: (415) 479-9722

Carol Stone
President/CEO
Volunteer Center of
    Greater Orange County
1000 East Santa Ana Boulevard
Suite 200
Santa Ana, CA 92701
Phone: (714) 953-5757
Fax: (714) 834-0585

Karen Delaney
Director
Volunteer Center of
    Santa Cruz County
1110 Emeline Avenue
Santa Cruz, CA 95060
Phone: (408) 423-0554
Fax: (408) 423-6267

Karen Johnson
Executive Director
Volunteer Center of Sonoma County
1041 Fourth Street
Santa Rosa, CA 95404
Phone: (707) 573-3399
Fax: (707) 573-3380

Veray Wickham
Director
Volunteer Center of

United Way/San Joaquin
P.O. Box 1585
Stockton, CA 95201
Phone: (209) 943-0870
Fax: (209) 943-7312

De De Hicks
Director
Volunteer Center
South Bay—Harbor—Long Beach
1230 Cravens Avenue
Torrance, CA 90501
Phone: (310) 212-7086
Fax: (310) 212-7201

Janet Osman
Director
Tulare Volunteer Bureau, Inc.
115 South "M" Street
Tulare, CA 93274
Phone: (209) 688-0539
Fax: (209) 687-1724

Martin Bradley
Director
Volunteer Center of
    Mendocino County
505 South State Street
Ukiah, CA 95482
Phone: (707) 462-8879

Renée Mason
Director
Volunteer Center of Victor Valley
15561 Seventh Street
Victorville, CA 92392
Phone: (619) 245-8592

Ed Jost
Director
Visalia Volunteer Service Program
310 North Locust
Visalia, CA 93291
Phone: (209) 730-7042
Fax: (209) 627-9155

COLORADO
Barbara Peterson
Director
Center for Information &
    Voluntary Action (CIVA)
400 East Main Street
Aspen, CO 81611
Phone: (303) 925-7887
Fax: (303) 920-2892

Marcella Bradley
Director
Volunteer Connection
3305 North Broadway, Suite 1
Boulder, CO 80304
Phone: (303) 444-4904

Robert D. Ridgeway
Director
Volunteer Center, Mile High
    United Way
2505 18th Street
Denver, CO 80211-3939
Phone: (303) 433-6060
Fax: (303) 455-6462

Jeannine Truswell
Director
Volunteer Resource Bureau of
    United Way
P.O. Box 1944
Greeley, CO 80632-1944
Phone: (303) 353-4300
Fax: (303) 353-4738

CONNECTICUT
State Office:
Deborah Walsh
Director
Volunteer Center of United Way of
    the Capital Area
99 Woodland Street
Hartford, CT 06105
Phone: (203) 247-2580
Fax: (203) 247-7949

Pat Tarasovic
Director
Valley Volunteer Action Center
75 Liberty Street
P.O. Box 418
Ansonia, CT 06401
Phone: (203) 732-8831
Fax: (203) 732-8831

Donna Marino
Director
United Way of
    Eastern Fairfield County
75 Washington Avenue
Bridgeport, CT 06604
Phone: (203) 334-5106
Fax: (203) 334-3297

Janice W. Martin
Interim Coordinator
Volunteer Center of
    Greater Bridgeport
P.O. Box 999
10 Middle Street
Bridgeport, CT 06601
Phone: (203) 335-3800
Fax: (203) 366-0105

Bobbi K. Feinson
Director
Volunteer Bureau of
    Greater Danbury
337 Main Street
Danbury, CT 06810
Phone: (203) 797-1154
Fax: (203) 790-5182

Elaine Tedesco
Director
Volunteer Action Center of
    Greater New Haven
70 Audubon Street
New Haven, CT 06510-1206
Phone: (203) 785-1997
Fax: (203) 787-6584

Margaret O'Brien
Director
Voluntary Action Center of
    Mid-Fairfield
83 East Avenue, Suite 307
Norwalk, CT 06851
Phone: (203) 852-0850
Fax: (203) 852-9357

Voluntary Action Center of
    South East Connecticut
12 Case Street, Suite 302
Norwich, CT 06360
Phone: (203) 887-2519

Ethelmarie Hunter
Director
Volunteer Center of
    Southwestern Fairfield County
62 Palmer's Hill Road
Stamford, CT 06902
Phone: (203) 348-7714
Fax: (203) 967-9507

DISTRICT OF COLUMBIA
State Office:
Christopher Murphy
Youth Voice Officer
Commission on National and
    Community Service
529 14th Street NW, Suite 452
Washington, DC 20045
Phone: (202) 724-0600
Fax: (202) 724-0608

James Lindsay
Executive Director
Washington Clearinghouse of
    District of Columbia
1313 New York Avenue NW, #303
Washington, DC 20005
Phone: (202) 638-2664
Fax: (202) 393-5365

DELAWARE
State Offices:
Marilyn Lavine

Director
State Office of Volunteer Links
1901 North Dupont Highway
New Castle, DE 19720
Phone: (302) 577-6420

Cynthia B. Lovell
Administrator
State Office of Volunteerism
Jesse Cooper Building
P.O. Box 637
Dover, DE 19903-0637
Phone: (302) 739-4456
Fax: (302) 739-6281

FLORIDA
State Offices:
Lee Whitney
Special Projects Director
Volunteer Services of Florida
Department of Health &
    Rehabilitation
1317 Winewood Road
Building 1, Room 210
Tallahassee, FL 32399-0700
Phone: (904) 488-2761
Fax: (904) 488-4227

Chris Gilmore
Special Assistant to the Governor
Office of the Governor
The Capitol
Tallahassee, FL 32399-0001

Janet Krause
Director
Manatee County Volunteer
    Services, Inc.
1701 14th Street West, Suite 2
Bradenton, FL 34205
Phone: (813) 746-7117
Fax: (813) 747-4519

Judy McGinty
Director
Volunteer Center for United Way
1149 Lake Drive
Cocoa, FL 32922

Phone: (407) 631-2740
Fax: (407) 631-2740

Dawn Arline
Director
United Way of Citrus County
P.O. Box 1379
Crystal River, FL 34223
Phone: (904) 795-8844

Mary L. Welch
Director
Volunteer Center of
    Volusia & Flagler Counties
West International Speedway Blvd.
Daytona Beach, FL 32124-1011
Phone: (904) 253-0563
Fax: (904) 253-0563 x253

Marilyn M. Mayhill
Director
Volunteer Broward
P.O. Box 22877
Fort Lauderdale, FL 33335
Phone: (305) 522-6761
Fax: (305) 462-4877

Jean Pennistan
Director
Voluntary Action Center of
    Lee County
6309 Corporate Court
P.O. Box 061039
Fort Myers, FL 33906
Phone: (813) 433-5301

Cathy Jenkins
Director
Volunteer Center of
    Alachua County, Inc.
P.O. Box 14561
Gainesville, FL 32601
Phone: (904) 378-2552
Fax: (904) 371-0018

Perry Heath
President
United Way of Central Florida
    Volunteer Center

P.O. Box 1357
Highland City, FL 33846-1357
Phone: (813) 648-1500
Fax: (813) 648-1535

Sarah Monroe
Director
Volunteer Jacksonville, Inc.
1600 Prudential Drive
Jacksonville, FL 32207
Phone: (904) 398-7777
Fax: (904) 346-4438

Rae Miller
Director
United Way of Munroe County
P.O. Box 1616
Key West, FL 33041
Phone: (305) 296-3464

Tanya Vajk
Director
United Way's Center for Volunteerism
1 South East Third Avenue
Suite 1950
Miami, FL 33101-0790
Phone: (305) 579-2300
Fax: (305) 579-2212

Susan Foster
Coordinator
Volunteer Center of Collier County
RSVP Center
811 Serenton Avenue South
Naples, FL 33940
Phone: (813) 263-3671
Fax: (813) 263-3430

Karen M. Ruble
Director
Volunteer Service Bureau of
    Marion County, Inc.
520 Southeast Fort King Street
Suite C-1
Ocala, FL 32671
Phone: (904) 732-4771
Fax: (904) 867-5933

Virginia Bowman
Executive Director
Volunteer Center of Central Florida
1900 North Mills Avenue, Suite 1
Orlando, FL 32803
Phone: (407) 896-0945
Fax: (407) 895-4749

Gretchen Stephenson
Director
United Way of Northwest Florida
P.O. Box 586
Panama City, FL 32402
Phone: (904) 769-2738

Judith W. Merritt
Director
Volunteer Pensacola
Voluntary Action Center, Inc.
7 North Coyle Street
Pensacola, FL 32501
Phone: (904) 438-5649

Jackie Lineberger
Director
Volunteer Center of Sarasota
1750 17th Street, #C-3
Sarasota, FL 34234
Phone: (813) 953-5965

Ann Breidenstein
Director
The Volunteer Center
P.O. Box 625
St. Augustine, FL 32085
Phone: (904) 829-9721

Dianna King
Director
Family Resources Volunteer Services
P.O. Box 13087
St. Petersburg, FL 33733
Phone: (813) 526-1100
Fax: (813) 527-1646

Francine Seminari
Director
United Way Volunteer Center
50 Kindred Street, Suite 207

P.O. Box 362
Stuart, FL 34995
Phone: (407) 220-1717
Fax: (407) 220-7771

Parker Cape
Director
Volunteer Service Center
United Way Big Ben
307 East Seventh Avenue
Tallahassee, FL 32303
Phone: (904) 222-6263

Betty Trimble
Director
Volunteer Center of Hillsborough
    County
P.O. Box 17229
Tampa, FL 33672-0249
Phone: (813) 221-8657
Fax: (813) 228-9549

Sharron Wilkin
Director
Volunteer Center South
400 Tamiami Trail South
Suite 230
Venice, FL 34285-2624
Phone: (813) 488-5683

Sue Schlitt
Director
United Way of Indian River
P.O. Box 1960
Vero Beach, FL 32961-1960
Phone: (407) 567-8900

Lyn Williams Mintle
Director
Volunteer Bureau of United Way
P.O. Box 20809
West Palm Beach, FL 33416-0809
Phone: (407) 820-2550
Fax: (407) 832-7947

GEORGIA
State Office:
Jim Marshall

Senior Coordinator
Georgia Office of Volunteer Services
1200 Equitable Building
100 Peachtree NW
Atlanta, GA 30303
Phone: (404) 656-9790
Fax: (404) 656-9792

Lagene Gruan
Director
Volunteer Albany
P.O. Box 7
Albany, GA 31702
Phone: (912) 883-6700
Fax: (912) 436-6378

Renée Dixon
Director
Volunteer Center
United Way of Metropolitan Atlanta
100 Edgewood Avenue NE
Suite 304
Atlanta, GA 30303
Phone: (404) 527-7346
Fax: (404) 527-7444

LaVerne H. Gold
Director
United Way of
    CSRA's Volunteer Center
630 Ellis Street
P.O. Box 30903
Augusta, GA 30901
Phone: (404) 826-4484
Fax: (404) 826-4462

Cathy J. Talley
Director
Voluntary Action Center
Hand-Up, Inc.
P.O. Box 631
Calhoun, GA 30703
Phone: (404) 629-7283

Lisa Keeble Von
Director
Volunteer Center
P.O. Box 1157

Columbus, GA 31902
Phone: (706) 596-8657
Fax: (706) 571-2271

Patsy B. Batson
Director
Voluntary Action Center of
    Northwest Georgia
P.O. Box 1941
305 South Thornton Avenue
Dalton, GA 30722-1941
Phone: (706) 226-4357
Fax: (706) 278-7994

Dottie Rigby
Director
Volunteer Gainesville
P.O. Box 1193
Gainesville, GA 30503
Phone: (706) 535-5445

Janet B. Frost
Director
Volunteer Macon
2484 Ingleside Avenue, Suite A-103
Macon, GA 31204
Phone: (912) 742-6677

James Burke
Executive Director
The Sharing Center, Inc.
P.O. Box 967
Newnan, GA 30264
Phone: (404) 304-1634
Fax: (404) 254-8497

Harold Boyd
Director
Floyd College Volunteer Center
P.O. Box 1864
Rome, GA 30162-1864
Phone: (706) 295-6335
Fax: (706) 295-6610

Audrey Fleming
Director
Voluntary Action Center of
    United Way
P.O. Box 9119

Savannah, GA 31412
Phone: (912) 234-1636
Fax: (912) 238-0281

Debbie Olds
Director
Volunteer Houston County
P.O. Box 266
Warner Robins, GA 31099-0266
Phone: (912) 953-9333

HAWAII
State Office:
Liane Kam
Program Coordinator
Hawaii Statewide
    Volunteer Services
Office of the Governor
P.O. Box 3375
Honolulu, HI 96801
Phone: (808) 587-2860
Fax: (808) 524-4389

Joan Naguwa
Director
Voluntary Action Center of Oahu
680 Iwilei, Suite 430
Honolulu, HI 96817
Phone: (808) 536-7234

IDAHO
Sharlene Brown
Director
United Way Volunteer Connection
5420 Franklin Road, Suite D
Boise, ID 83705
Phone: (208) 345-4357

ILLINOIS
State Office:
Allyson Zedler
Director
Office of Volunteer Action
Office of Lieutenant Governor
100 West Randolph, Suite 1500
Chicago, IL 60601

Phone: (312) 814-5220
Fax: (312) 814-4862

Richard Reed
Director
Volunteer Center of
    Northwest Suburban Chicago
306 West Park Street
Arlington Heights, IL 60005
Phone: (708) 398-1320
Fax: (708) 398-1128

Laurie Diekhoff
Director
Volunteer Center of United Way of
    McLean County
201 East Grove Street
P.O. Box 3605
Bloomington, IL 61702
Phone: (309) 829-2469
Fax: (309) 827-7485

Susan Norris
Manager, Center for Volunteerism
Volunteer Center
United Way/Crusade of Mercy
560 West Lake Street
Chicago, IL 60661-1499
Phone: (312) 906-2425
Fax: (312) 876-0721

Frank French
President/CEO
Volunteer Network
300 West Washington, Suite 1414
Chicago, IL 60606
Phone: (312) 606-8240
Fax: (312) 201-3554

Ronda Bollwahn
Director
Volunteer Center of Salvation Army
10 West Algonquin
Volunteer Services Bureau
Des Plaines, IL 60016
Phone: (708) 294-2116
Fax: (708) 294-2299

Barbara B. Pingrey
Director
Volunteer Center of Knox County
140 East Main Street
Galesburg, IL 61401
Phone: (309) 343-4434

Caren Vollrath
Director
Volunteer Center for Lake County
2020 O'Plaine Road
Green Oaks, IL 60048
Phone: (708) 816-0063
Fax: (708) 816-0093

Evelyn E. Craig
Director
Volunteer Center of
    Greater Quad Cities
1417 6th Avenue
Moline, IL 61265
Phone: (309) 764-6804
Fax: (309) 764-2415

Patricia Chapel
Director
Volunteer Center of United Way of
    Champaign County
1802 Woodfield Drive
P.O. Box 44
Savoy, IL 61874
Phone: (217) 352-5151
Fax: (217) 352-6494

Lila G. Christensen
Director
Community Volunteer Center
Lincoln Land Community College
Shepherd Road
Springfield, IL 62794-9256
Phone: (217) 786-2430
Fax: (217) 786-2251

Thomas Zucker
Director
Voluntary Action Center
1606 Bethany Road
Sycamore, IL 60178

Phone: (815) 758-3932

Valerie A. Bruggeman
Director
Volunteer Center of DuPage
421 North County Farm Road
Wheaton, IL 60185
Phone: (708) 682-7507
Fax: (708) 682-7382

INDIANA
State Office:
Judy Wood McKillip
Director
Governor's Voluntary Action Program
Indiana Government Center South
302 West Washington, Room E-220
Indianapolis, IN 46204
Phone: (317) 232-2504
Fax: (317) 232-1815

Beth Neu
Director
Bloomington Voluntary
    Action Center
P.O. Box 100
Bloomington, IN 47402
Phone: (812) 331-6430

Elizabeth Clark
Executive Director
First Call For Help Volunteer Services
P.O. Box 827
Columbus, IN 47202
Phone: (812) 376-0011
Fax: (812) 376-0019

Kathy Fox
Director
United Way Volunteer Action Center
P.O. Box 18
101 NW First Street, Suite 215
Evansville, IN 47701
Phone: (812) 421-2801
Fax: (812) 421-7474

Judi Lee
Program Manager

Volunteer Connection
227 East Washington Boulevard
Fort Wayne, IN 46802
Phone: (219) 420-4263
Fax: (219) 424-4999

Daniel L. Harer
Director
The Window Community
    Volunteer Center
223 S. Main Street
Goshen, IN 46526
Phone: (219) 533-9680

Robert MacConnell
President
Human Resources Department of
    United Way
221 West Ridge Road
Griffith, IN 46319
Phone: (219) 923-2302
Fax: (219) 923-8601

Martha Bolyard
Director
United Way Volunteer Action Center
United Way of Central Indiana
3901 North Meridian Street, Suite 25
Indianapolis, IN 46208-4041
Phone: (317) 912-1275
Fax: (317) 921-1355

Marilyn McIntosh
Executive Director
Volunteer Action Center
Volunteers & Community Service
210 West Walnut Street
Kokomo, IN 46901-4512
Phone: (317) 457-4481
Fax: (317) 454-5572

Marcile Eddy
Director
Greater Lafayette Volunteer
    Bureau, Inc.
301 ½ Columbia Street
Lafayette, IN 47901
Phone: (317) 742-8241

Shelly Lindsay
Director
Community Resource Center of
    St. Joseph
914 Lincolnway West
South Bend, IN 46616
Phone: (219) 232-2522

Linnie Wade
Vice President, Community Outreach
United Way's Community
    Volunteer Service
United Way of St. Joseph County
3517 East Jefferson
South Bend, IN 46660-0396
Phone: (219) 232-8201
Fax: (219) 232-2350

Julie Young
Executive Director
Volunteer Action Center
721 Wabash Avenue, Suite 502
Terre Haute, IN 47807
Phone: (812) 232-8822

IOWA
State Office:
Barbara Finch
Director
Governor's Office of Volunteers
State Capitol
Des Moines, IA 50319
Phone: (515) 281-8304
Fax: (515) 281-6611

Charene Starcevic
Director
Volunteer Center of Story County
510 Fifth Street
Ames, IA 50010
Phone: (515) 232-2736

Kathy Vigil
Director
United Way of East Central Iowa
1030 5th Avenue SE
Cedar Rapids, IA 52403
Phone: (319) 398-5372

Marcia Antworth
Director
Volunteer Bureau of Council Bluffs
523 6th Avenue
Council Bluffs, IA 51503
Phone: (712) 322-6431

Jane Kieler
Senior Director,
Community Services
United Way of Central Iowa
   Volunteer Center
1111 Ninth Street, Suite 300
Des Moines, IA 50314
Phone: (515) 246-6542
Fax: (515) 246-6546

Sally Stutsman
Director
Volunteer Action Center
20 East Market
Iowa City, IA 52245
Phone: (319) 338-7823

Katrina Wisniewski
Director
Voluntary Action Center of
   Muscatine
415 East 2nd Street
Muscatine, IA 52761
Phone: (319) 263-0959

Joan McCulloch
Director
Voluntary Action Center of Iowa
   Great Lakes
1713 Hill Avenue
Spirit Lake, IA 51360
Phone: (712) 336-4444

Robin Mueller
Community Resources Coordinator
United Way Volunteer Center
c/o Cedar Valley United Way
3420 University Avenue, Suite C
Waterloo, IA 50707
Phone: (319) 235-6211
Fax: (319) 233-6963

KANSAS
State Office:
Pat Kells
Executive Director
Kansas Office for Community
   Service
P.O. Box 889
Topeka, KS 66601
Phone: (913) 575-8330

Debbie Berndsen
Director
Reno County Retired Senior
   Volunteer Program & VAC
1300 North Plum
Hutchinson, KS 67501
Phone: (316) 665-3566

Jean Nelson
Director
Wyandotte County Volunteer
   Center
P.O. Box 17-1042
Kansas City, KS 66117
Phone: (913) 371-3674
Fax: (913) 371-2718

Lanaea Heine
Director
Roger Hill Volunteer Center
P.O. Box 116
Lawrence, KS 66044
Phone: (913) 865-5030
Fax: (913) 843-6752

Donna Malone
Director
Volunteer Center of Johnson
   County
6900 West 80, Suite 300
Overland Park, KS 66204-3839
Phone: (913) 341-1792
Fax: (913) 341-7077

Nancy Klestermeyer
Director
RSVP/The Volunteer Center
236 North 7th, Suite B

Salina, KS 67401
Phone: (913) 823-3128
Fax: (913) 827-9321

Patsy Congrove
Director
Volunteer Center of Topeka
4125 Gage Center Drive, Suite 214
Topeka, KS 66604
Phone: (913) 272-8890

Mary Knecht
Director
Rotary Volunteers in Action
300 West Douglas #1000
Wichita, KS 67202
Phone: (316) 267-7842
Fax: (316) 262-5101

Lori Zulfigar
Director
United Way Volunteer Center
212 North Market, Suite 200
Wichita, KS 67202
Phone: (316) 261-1321
Fax: (316) 267-0937

KENTUCKY
State Office:
Norma W. Johnson
Executive Director
Kentucky Office of Volunteer Services
275 East Main Street, 6W
Frankfort, KY 40621-0001
Phone: (502) 564-4357
Fax: (502) 564-3096

Rachael A. Mullins
Coordinator
Volunteer Center of Bowling Green
—Warren County
P.O. Box 1320
Bowling Green, KY 42102-1320
Phone: (502) 842-4281

Glenda A. Guess
Executive Director
Volunteer & Information Center

236 North Elm Street
P.O. Box 2009
Henderson, KY 42420
Phone: (502) 831-2273
Fax: (502) 826-2111

Becky Ewalt
Executive Director
Volunteer Center of The Bluegrass
2029 Bellefonte Drive
Lexington, KY 40503
Phone: (606) 278-6258
Fax: (606) 278-4435

Libby Marquardt
Director
Volunteer Connection
334 East Broadway
P.O. Box 4488
Louisville, KY 40204-0488
Phone: (502) 583-2821
Fax: (502) 583-0330

Dan Douglas
Executive Director
Volunteer Center of Owensboro-
    Davies County, Inc.
P.O. Box 506
Owensboro, KY 42302
Phone: (502) 683-9161
Fax: (502) 926-2825

Sandy Williamson
Director
Volunteer Center
Big Sandy Area Development
    District
503 South Lake Drive
Prestonsburg, KY 41653
Phone: (606) 886-2374
Fax: (606) 886-3382 x336

Vickie L. Bailey
Director
Kentucky River Foothills
    Development Council, Inc.
Volunteer Resource Center
110 South Collins Street

P.O. Box 74
Richmond, KY 40476-0743
Phone: (606) 624-2046
Fax: (606) 624-2049

LOUISIANA
State Office:
Sally King
Director of Volunteers
Office of the Governor
State Capitol Building
Baton Rouge, LA 70804

Noel B. Parnell
Director
Volunteer Baton Rouge
4962 Florida Boulevard, Suite 412
Baton Rouge, LA 70806-4031
Phone: (504) 927-8270
Fax: (504) 926-3076

Michael Blanchard
Director
Volunteer Center of Lafayette
1120 Coolidge Boulevard
Lafayette, LA 70503
Phone: (318) 233-1006
Fax: (318) 232-3371

Beverly S. McCormick
Director
Volunteer Center of
    Southwest Louisiana
834 Ryan Street, Suite 401
Lake Charles, LA 70601
Phone: (318) 439-6109
Fax: (318) 478-0017

Sydney Heard
Executive Director
United Way of Northeast Louisiana
1300 Hudson Lane, Suite 7
Monroe, LA 71201
Phone: (318) 325-3869
Fax: (318) 325-4329

Gail McGlothin
Director

Volunteer & Information Agency
4747 Earhart Boulevard, Suite 111
New Orleans, LA 70125
Phone: (504) 488-4636
Fax: (504) 482-6511

MAINE
Barbara K. Wentworth
Director
Volunteer! York County
36 Water Street, Unit C
Kennebunk, ME 04043
Phone: (207) 985-6869
Fax: (207) 985-3564

Susan H. Hornbeck
Director
United Way Volunteer Center
233 Oxford Street
P.O. Box 3820
Portland, ME 04104-3820
Phone: (207) 874-1000
Fax: (207) 874-1007

MARYLAND
State Office:
David A. Minges
Director
Governor's Office on Volunteerism
301 West Preston Street, Suite 1501
Baltimore, MD 21201
Phone: (301) 225-4496
Fax: (301) 333-7124

Karen Henry
Coordinator
Anne Arundel County
Office of Community Services
P.O. Box 2700
Arundel Center, Room 230
Annapolis, MD 21404
Phone: (410) 222-1530
Fax: (410) 222-1575

Jeannine Myers
Coordinator
Volunteer Center of

Federick County, Maryland
22 South Market Street
Frederick, MD 21701
Phone: (301) 663-9096

Mary L. Reese
Executive Director
Prince Georges' Voluntary Action
    Center, Inc.
6309 Baltimore Avenue, Suite 305
Riverdale, MD 20737
Phone: (301) 779-9444

Jim Johnson
Director
Montgomery County Volunteer &
    Community Service Center
401 Fleet Street #104
Rockville, MD 20850-2621
Phone: (301) 217-4949

MASSACHUSETTS
State Office:
Joanne Patton
Director
State Office for Volunteerism
Commonwealth of Massachusetts
650 Asbury Street
Hamilton, MA 01982
Phone: (508) 468-3720
Fax: (508) 468-7604

Bette Rossen
Assistant Vice President
Community Services
    Voluntary Action Center
United Way of Massachusetts Bay
2 Liberty Square
Boston, MA 02109-4844
Phone: (617) 422-6765
Fax: (617) 482-6021

Nancy Harding
Director
Volunteer Service Center
United Way
P.O. Box 7823

New Bedford, MA 02742
Phone: (508) 994-9625
Fax: (508) 999-7220

Donna R. Nelson-Ivy
Director
Voluntary Action Center
184 Mill Street
P.O. Box 3040
Springfield, MA 01102-3040
Phone: (413) 737-2691
Fax: (413) 788-4131

Barbara LaFrance
Director
Volunteer Bureau of United Way of
    Greater Taunton
4 Court Street
P.O. Box 416
Taunton, MA 02780
Phone: (508) 824-3985

Hermia Salisbury
Coordinator
Volunteer Center of Franklin
    County
c/o Franklin County Home Care
    Corporation
58 Main Street
Turners Falls, MA 01376
Phone: (413) 773-5555
Fax: (413) 772-1084

Jean Strock
Director
Volunteer Center
United Way of Central Massachusetts
484 Main Street
Worcester, MA 01608
Phone: (508) 757-5631
Fax: (508) 757-2712

MICHIGAN
State Office:
Diana Algra
Executive Director
Michigan Community Services

Commission
111 S. Capital Avenue
Olds Plaza, 4th Floor
Lansing, MI 48909
Phone: (517) 335-4295
Fax: (517) 373-4977

Christine MacNaughton
Coordinator
Volunteer Center of Lenawee
104 East Maumee, Suite 1
Adrian, MI 49221
Phone: (517) 263-4696
Fax: (517) 265-3039

Mark Lelle
Director
The Albion Volunteer Service Center
203 South Superior Street
Albion, MI 49224
Phone: (517) 629-5574

Vernie Nethercut
Director
Alpena Volunteer Center of Alpena
    Community College
666 Johnson Street
Alpena, MI 49707
Phone: (517) 356-9021 x271
Fax: (517) 356-6334

Mary Field
Manager for Information and
    Referral Division
Washtenaw United Way
Volunteer Action Center
P.O. Box 3813
Ann Arbor, MI 48106
Phone: (313) 971-5852
Fax: (313) 971-6230

Carolyn Harvey
Director
Volunteer Bureau of Battle Creek
182 West Van Buren Street
Battle Creek, MI 49017
Phone: (616) 965-0555
Fax: (616) 966-4194

Megan Corbett
Executive Director
Volunteer Action Center of
    Bay County, Inc.
315 Fourteenth Street
Bay City, MI 48708-7148
Phone: (517) 893-6060
Fax: (517) 893-6073

Patricia Christie
Community Services Director
Thumb Volunteer Center
Human Development Commission
429 Montague Avenue
Caro, MI 48723
Phone: (517) 673-4121
Fax: (517) 673-2031

Maurice P. Wesson
Senior Manager
Center for Volunteerism
United Community Services of
    Metropolitan Detroit
1212 Griswold
Detroit, MI 48226-1899
Phone: (313) 226-9429
Fax: (313) 226-9397

Sybyl Atwood
Director
Volunteer Center
United Way of Genesee & Lapeer
202 East Boulevard Drive
Flint, MI 48503
Phone: (313) 232-8121
Fax: (313) 232-9370

Ethel A. Kage
Coordinator
Volunteer Connection
The United Way
500 Commerce Building
Grand Rapids, MI 49503-3165
Phone: (616) 459-6281
Fax: (616) 459-8460

John Niemela
Director

Voluntary Action Center of
  Keweenaw
606 Quincy Street
Hancock, MI 49930

Glenda McKinley
Director
Greater Holland United Way
70 West Eighth Street
P.O. Box 20809
Holland, MI 49423
Phone: (616) 396-7811
Fax: (616) 396-5140

Jennifer Meyer
Director
Livingston County United Way
3780 East Grand River
Howell, MI 48843
Phone: (517) 546-4612

Aaron Cantrell
Director
Voluntary Action Center of
  Greater Kalamazoo
709-A South Westnedge
Kalamazoo, MI 49007
Phone: (616) 382-8350
Fax: (616) 382-8362

Sharon Radtke
Director
Voluntary Action Center of
  Greater Lansing
6035 Executive Drive, Suite 105
Lansing, MI 48911
Phone: (517) 887-8004

Sally Terrill
Director
Voluntary Action Center of
  Midland County, Inc.
Strosacker Center
220 West Main Street, Suite 103
Midland, MI 48640-5137
Phone: (517) 631-7660
Fax: (517) 832-5526

C. DeWayne Duskin
Executive Director
United Way's First Call for
  Help/VAC
6 South Monroe Street
Monroe, MI 48161-2280
Phone: (313) 242-3378
Fax: (313) 242-1331

Norman Cunningham
Director
Volunteer Center of
  Muskegon County
2525 Hall Road
Muskegon, MI 49442
Phone: (616) 777-3806

Kathryn S. Rossow
Director
Southwestern Michigan Volunteer
  Center—Niles Branch
1213 Oak Street
Niles, MI 49120
Phone: (616) 683-5464
Fax: (616) 683-5470

Eve E. Gohlke
Director
Voluntary Action Center
118 East Genesee
Saginaw, MI 48607
Phone: (517) 755-2822

Kathryn S. Rossow
Director
Southwestern Michigan Volunteer
  Center—St. Joseph Branch
508 Pleasant Street
St. Joseph, MI 49085
Phone: (616) 983-0912

MINNESOTA
State Office:
Paula J. Beugen
Director

Minnesota Office on
Volunteer Services
500 Rice Street
St. Paul, MN 55155
Phone: (612) 296-4731
Fax: (612) 297-8260

Marsha Eisenberg
Director
Voluntary Action Center
402 Ordean Building
424 West Superior Street
Duluth, MN 55802
Phone: (218) 726-4776
Fax: (218) 726-4778

Cindy Tyner
Director
United Way's Voluntary
Action Center
404 South 8th Street
Minneapolis, MN 55404
Phone: (612) 340-7537
Fax: (612) 340-7675

Lois McDougall
Director
Volunteer Connection, Inc.
903 West Center Street, Suite 200
Rochester, MN 55902
Phone: (507) 287-2244
Fax: (507) 287-2063

Kathleen Jowett
Director
Voluntary Action Center of
St. Paul Area, Inc.
251 Starkey Street, Suite 127
St. Paul, MN 55107-1821
Phone: (612) 227-3938
Fax: (612) 223-8139

Kathy Miron
Director
Community Volunteer Center of
St. Croix Valley
2300 West Orlin Street

Stillwater, MN 55082
Phone: (612) 439-7434

MISSISSIPPI
Henrietta Ramsey
Coordinator
Volunteer Resource Center
P.O. Box 23169
Jackson, MS 39225-3169
Phone: (601) 354-1765
Fax: (601) 968-8596

Karen Webb
Coordinator
Volunteer Jackson County
3510 Magnolia Street
Pascagoula, MS 39568-0097
Phone: (601) 762-8557
Fax: (601) 762-7669

Beverly Shelton
Executive Director
Volunteer Center
P.O. Box 1053
Tupelo, MS 38802
Phone: (601) 844-8989
Fax: (601) 844-8254

MISSOURI
State Office:
Jeannie Kraeger
President
Missouri Volunteers
Malcomb Bliss Mental Health
5400 Arsenal Street
St. Louis, MO 63139
Phone: (314) 644-7800
Fax: (314) 644-7898

Cindy Mustard
Executive Director
Voluntary Action Center
111 South Ninth, Suite 200
Columbia, MO 65201
Phone: (314) 449-6959

Mary Hutchison
Director
Voluntary Action Center of
    Eastern Jackson County
10901 Winner Road, Suite 102
Independence, MO 64052
Phone: (816) 252-2636

Pat Cundiff
Director
Heart of America
United Way Volunteer Center
1080 Washington Street, Suite 204
Kansas City, MO 64105
Phone: (816) 474-5112
Fax: (816) 472-4207

Reba Condra
Director
Voluntary Action Center
P.O. Box 188
St. Joseph, MO 64502-0188
Phone: (816) 364-2381
Fax: (816) 364-6030

Barbara J. Henning
Director
United Way of Greater St. Louis
Voluntary Action Center
1111 Olive
St. Louis, MO 63101
Phone: (314) 421-0700
Fax: (314) 539-4154

MONTANA
Sandi Filipowicz
Executive Director
Community Help Line
113 6th Street North
Great Falls, MT 59401
Phone: (406) 761-6010

NEBRASKA
State Office:
Pat Taft
Director
Nebraska Department of Social Services

301 Centennial Mall South
Lincoln, NE 68509
Phone: (402) 471-9107
Fax: (402) 471-9449

Jamesena Grimes Moore
Director
United Way Volunteer Bureau
Volunteer Action Center
1805 Harney Street
Omaha, NE 68102-1972
Phone: (402) 342-8232
Fax: (402) 342-7402

Evelyn Pinneker
Director
Scottsbluff County
Volunteer Bureau
1721 Broadway, Room 409
Scottsbluff, NE 69361
Phone: (308) 632-3736

NEVADA
Jacqueline Matthews
Director
United Way Volunteer Center
1660 East Flamingo
Las Vegas, NV 89119-5254
Phone: (702) 734-2273
Fax: (702) 734-8504

Tom Jacobs
Director of Resource Development
United Way of Northern Nevada &
    Sierra Volunteer Center
P.O. Box 2730
Reno, NV 89505-2730
Phone: (702) 322-8668
Fax: (702) 322-2798

NEW HAMPSHIRE
State Office:
Kathleen J. Desmarais
Executive Director
Governor's Office on Volunteerism
The State House Annex, Room 409
25 Capitol Street

Concord, NH 03301
Phone: (603) 271-3771
Fax: (603) 271-2130

Martha Bauman
Director
Monadnock Volunteer Center
331 Maine Street
Keene, NH 03431
Phone: (603) 352-2088
Fax: (603) 357-6859

Betty Cote
Program Manager
Voluntary Action Center
102 N. Main Street
Manchester, NH 03102
Phone: (603) 668-8601

NEW JERSEY
State Office:
Anna Thomas
Director
New Jersey Office of Volunteerism
Department of Human Services
CN 700
Trenton, NJ 08625
Phone: (609) 292-4497
Fax: (609) 292-6838

Maggie Sadler
Director
Volunteer Center of
    Hunterdon County
14 Route 31
Annandale, NJ 08801
Phone: (908) 735-4357
Fax: (908) 735-9353

Curtis Morris
Director
The SkillsBank
Northgage I
7th & Linden Streets, First floor
Camden, NJ 08102
Phone: (609) 541-3939
Fax: (609) 964-6152

Marguerite Logan
Director
Volunteer Center of
    Bergen County, Inc.
64 Passaic Street
Hackensack, NJ 07601
Phone: (201) 489-9454
Fax: (201) 489-1995

Joan McKinsey
Director
Volunteer Services Center
32 Ford Avenue
Milltown, NJ 08850
Phone: (908) 247-3727
Fax: (908) 247-9855

Jean R. Gleason
Director
Voluntary Action Center of
    Morris County
36 South Street
Morristown, NJ 07960
Phone: (201) 538-7200

Joyce Wibbelt
Director
Volunteer Center of
    Greater Essex County
303-9 Washington Street
Newark, NJ 07102
Phone: (201) 622-3737

Joanne Drane
Director
Volunteer Center of Atlantic County
P.O. Box 648
Northfield, NJ 08225
Phone: (609) 272-2488
Fax: (609) 272-2421

Joan Fisch
Interim Director
Volunteer Center of
    Greater Essex County
439 Main Street
Orange, NJ 07050
Phone: (201) 676-8899
Fax: (201) 676-5598

Charissa Murray
Director
Volunteer Action Center of
    Passaic County
2 Market Street, Fourth Floor
Paterson, NJ 07501
Phone: (201) 279-6526
Fax: (201) 279-0059

Claire Jones
Director
Volunteer Office
Medical Center of Ocean County
2121 Edgewater Place
Point Pleasant, NJ 08742
Phone: (908) 295-6372
Fax: (908) 892-2679

Maureen Miner
Director
Volunteer Center of
    Monmouth County
227 East Bergen Place
Red Bank, NJ 07701
Phone: (908) 741-3330
Fax: (908) 741-0110

Jill C. McConnell
Director
Volunteer Center of Somerset County
205 West Main Street, Fourth Floor
P.O. Box 308
Somerville, NJ 08876-0308
Phone: (908) 725-6640
Fax: (980) 725-5598

Carol Throne
Coordinator of Volunteer Services
Volunteer Center of Mercer County
3131 Princeton Pike, Building #4
Trenton, NJ 08601
Phone: (609) 896-1912
Fax: (609) 895-1245

NEW MEXICO
State Office:
Jeannette Miller
Director

Governor's Office
State Capitol
Santa Fe, NM 87503
Phone: (505) 827-3000
Fax: (505) 827-3026

Bruce Cline
Director
Volunteer Center of Albuquerque
P.O. Box 1767
Albuquerque, NM 87103
Phone: (505) 247-3671
Fax: (505) 242-3576

Anita Jenks
Office Manager
Volunteer Involvement Service
College of Santa Fe
Santa Fe, NM 87501
Phone: (505) 473-1000

NEW YORK
State Office:
Lou Trapani
Director
Governor's Office for
    Voluntary Services
2 World Trade Center, 57th Floor
New York, NY 10047
Phone: (212) 417-2255
Fax: (212) 417-4709

Audrey Kibrick
Director
Volunteer Center of Albany
100 State Street
Albany, NY 12207-1800
Phone: (518) 434-2061

Joyce Stafford
Director of Community Programs
Voluntary Action Center
United Way of Broome County, Inc.
P.O. Box 550
Binghamton, NY 13902-0550
Phone: (607) 729-2592
Fax: (607) 729-2597

Marilyn Wilson
Director of Agency Services
Volunteer Center
United Way of Buffalo/Erie County
742 Delaware Avenue
Buffalo, NY 14209
Phone: (716) 887-2632
Fax: (716) 882-0071

Nancy M. Cox
Director
Volunteer Connection
United Way of
   Southeast Stuben County
29 Denison Parkway East, Suite A
Corning, NY 14830
Phone: (607) 962-4644
Fax: (607) 936-4376

Rita Mahon Rath
Director
Voluntary Action Center of
   Glens Falls, Inc.
65 Ridge Street
Glens Falls, NY 12801
Phone: (518) 793-3817

Judith Brentley
Coordinator
Volunteer Service Bureau
United Way of South Chautaugua
413 North Main Street
Jamestown, NY 14701
Phone: (716) 483-1562

Winifred L. Brown
Director
Mayor's Voluntary Action Center
61 Chambers Street
New York, NY 10007
Phone: (212) 788-7550
Fax: (212) 406-3587

Evelyn Barosin
Director
Volunteer Center of Dutchess
County
9 Vassar Street

Poughkeepsie, NY 12603
Phone: (914) 452-5600

Thomas F. Toole & Ruth Seigel
Directors
Volunteer Resources Division
United Way of Greater Rochester
55 St. Paul Street
Rochester, NY 14604
Phone: (716) 454-2770
Fax: (716) 454-6568

Robert J. Marston
Director
Rome Voluntary Action Center
City Hall on the Mall
Rome, NY 13440
Phone: (315) 336-5638

Catherine Baycroft
Executive Director
Volunteer Action Center of
   Human Services
152 Barrett Street
Schenectady, NY 12305
Phone: (518) 372-3395

Jean J. Greene
Director
Volunteer Center of Syracuse &
   Onondaga County
115 East Jefferson Street, Suite 400
Phone: (315) 474-7011
Fax: (315) 479-6772

Jacqueline Mulligan
Director
Volunteer Center of
   Rensselaer County
272 River Street
Troy, NY 12180
Phone: (518) 272-1000

Nan Patterson
Director
Voluntary Action Center of
   Greater Utica, Inc.
1644 Genesee Street

Utica, NY 13502
Phone: (315) 735-4463

Mary Ellen Gimgerish
Director
Volunteer Center of Jefferson County
518 Davidson Street, Room 2
Watertown, NY 13601
Phone: (315) 788-0422

Bill Straubinger
Director
Volunteer Center of United Way
470 Mamaroneck Avenue, Room 204
White Plains, NY 10605
Phone: (914) 948-4452
Fax: (914) 948-3032

NORTH CAROLINA
State Office:
Dawn P. Lowder
Executive Director
Governor's Office of Citizen Affairs
116 West Jones Street
Raleigh, NC 27603-8001
Phone: (919) 733-2391
Fax: (919) 733-2120

Carol Nobles
Director
Volunteer Center of United Way
Asheville & Buncombe County
50 South French Broad Avenue
Asheville, NC 28801
Phone: (704) 255-0696
Fax: (704) 255-8004

Kathy M. Batton
Director
Moore County Volunteer Center
P.O. Box 905
Carthage, NC 28327
Phone: (919) 947-6395
Fax: (919) 947-1874

Lynn Wareh
Director
Volunteer Center of Orange County

P.O. Box 845
Chapel Hill, NC 27514
Phone: (919) 929-9837

Lisa Martinez
Director
Volunteer Center of United Way of
    Central Carolina
301 South Brevard Street
Charlotte, NC 28202
Phone: (704) 372-7170
Fax: (704) 342-4482

Anne N. Moore
Executive Director
Volunteer Center of Greater Durham
119 Orange Street
Durham, NC 27701
Phone: (919) 688-8977
Fax: (919) 688-7445

Sue Thomas
Director
Volunteer Center
P.O. Box 2001
Fayetteville, NC 28302
Phone: (919) 323-8643

Doris Shaw
Director
Volunteer Center of Wayne County
P.O. Box 1107
308 North William Street
Goldsboro, NC 27533
Phone: (919) 736-3344

Christine T. Greeson
Director
Voluntary Action Center
1500 Yanceyville Street
Greensboro, NC 27405
Phone: (919) 373-1633
Fax: (919) 378-1166

Nancy C. Gray
Director
Volunteer Center of Vance County, Inc.
P.O. Box 334

Henderson, NC 27536
Phone: (919) 492-5675

Lucy Purkey
Director
Volunteer Center of
    Henderson County
Opportunity House
1411 Asheville Highway
Hendersonville, NC 28739
Phone: (704) 692-8700

Gail Drum
Director
Volunteer Center
P.O. Box 2425
Hickory, NC 28603
Phone: (704) 324-4357
Fax: (704) 324-4358

Gayle Kearns
Director
United Way Volunteer Center of
    Greater High Point
305 North Main Street
High Point, NC 27260
Phone: (919) 883-6171
Fax: (919) 883-6928

Margaret Marchuk
Director
Dare Voluntary Action Center
P.O. Box 293
Manteo, NC 27954-0293
Phone: (919) 473-2400

Stephen Dudek
Director
United Way of Wake County
Voluntary Action Center
P.O. Box 11426
Raleigh, NC 27604
Phone: (919) 833-5739
Fax: (919) 833-5848

James H. Mack
Director
Volunteer Center of
    Richmond County

101 Rockingham Road
Rockingham, NC 28379
Phone: (919) 895-0130
Fax: (919) 895-6012

Anne Short
Director
United Way of Cleveland County
P.O. Box 2242
Shelby, NC 28150
Phone: (704) 482-7344
Fax: (704) 487-7458

Pete Barnett
Director
Volunteer & Information Center
P.O. Box 333
Supply, NC 28462
Phone: (919) 754-4766

Director
Volunteer Action Center of
    Haywood
1124 Sulphur Springs Road
Waynesville, NC 28786
Phone: (704) 456-4822

Twana Wellman
Director
Volunteer Center—United Way
P.O. Box 20669
Winston-Salem, NC 27120
Phone: (919) 723-3601
Fax: (919) 724-1045

Brenda Holbrook
Director
Yadkin County
Volunteer Action Center
P.O. Box 1053
106 Elm St.
Yadkinville, NC 27055
Phone: (919) 679-2071

NORTH DAKOTA
State Office:
Warren C. Enyart
Director

Economic Development and
   Finance Department
1833 East Bismarck Expressway
Bismarck, ND 58504
Phone: (701) 221-5330
Fax: (701) 221-5320

Jack Olson
Director
Missouri Slope Areawide United Way
P.O. Box 2111
Bismarck, ND 58502
Phone: (701) 255-3601
Fax: (701) 255-6243

Melinda Haun Hohncke
Director
Volunteer Center
Community Resources, Inc.
P.O. Box 1609
Fargo, ND 58107-1609
Phone: (701) 237-5050
Fax: (701) 237-0982

Nancy Martin
President
United Way Volunteer Center
P.O. Box 207
406 De Mers Avenue
Grand Forks, ND 58206-0207
Phone: (701) 775-0671
Fax: (701) 775-0672

OHIO
State Office:
Ruth Milligan
Special Assistant to the Governor
GIVE: Governor's Initiative on
   Volunteer Efforts
77 South High Street, 30th Floor
Columbus, OH 43215
Phone: (614) 644-0900
Fax: (614) 466-9354

Josie McElroy
Director
Volunteer Center of Summit

County
P.O. Box 4029
425 West Market
Akron, OH 44303-2044
Phone: (216) 762-8991
Fax: (216) 762-3121

Maria B. Heege
Director
United Way's Community &
   Volunteer Services
618 Second Street NW
Canton, OH 44703
Phone: (216) 453-9172
Fax: (216) 455-8909

Alice Sems
Director
Info-Line
Volunteer Bureau
107 Water Street
Chardon, OH 44024
Phone: (216) 285-3194
Fax: (216) 285-3442

Lucy Crane
Manager
Voluntary Action Center
United Appeal/Community Chest
2400 Reading Road
Cincinnati, OH 45202-1478
Phone: (513) 762-7192
Fax: (513) 762-7138

Martha M. Barber
Manager
Volunteer Center
United Way Services
3100 Euclid Avenue
Cleveland, OH 44115
Phone: (216) 881-3170
Fax: (216) 432-4863

Kitty Burcsu
Executive Director
CALLVAC Services
370 South Fifth Street
Columbus, OH 43215

Phone: (614) 221-6766
Fax: (614) 224-6866

Pamela Swaim
Director
Voluntary Action Center
United Way of Greater Dayton
184 Salem Avenue
Dayton, OH 45406-5877
Phone: (513) 225-3066
Fax: (513) 225-3074

David Fagerlie
Chief Professional Officer
United Way of Hancock County
Voluntary Action Center
124 West Front Street
Findlay, OH 45840
Phone: (419) 423-1432
Fax: (419) 423-4918

Karen Rossi
Volunteer Center Director
Voluntary Action Center
Warren County United Way
20 North Mechanic
Lebanon, OH 45036
Phone: (513) 932-3987
Fax: (513) 932-0214

B. Cheryl Casler
Director
Volunteer Center of Richland County
35 North Park Street
Mansfield, OH 44902-1711
Phone: (419) 525-2816
Fax: (419) 524-3467

Jeanne M. Hurt
Director
Medina County Organization on
   Volunteering
113 East Homestead Street
Medina, OH 44256
Phone: (216) 725-3926
Fax: (216) 725-3000

Mary L. Geoghan
Director

Volunteer Center in Huron County
258 Benedict Avenue
Shady Lane, Entrance 4
Norwalk, OH 44857
Phone: (419) 663-1179
Fax: (419) 663-0889-store

Kay Wright
Director
Volunteer Center of Erie County
108 West Shoreline Drive
Sandusky, OH 44870
Phone: (419) 627-0074
Fax: (419) 625-4673

Betty Payton
Director
Volunteer Service Bureau of Clark
   County, Inc.
616 North Limestone Street
Springfield, OH 45503
Phone: (513) 322-4262
Fax: (513) 324-2605

Christine Kolasinski
Director
Voluntary Action Center
United Way of Greater Toledo
1 Stranahan Square, Suite 141
Toledo, OH 43604
Phone: (419) 244-3063
Fax: (419) 246-4614

Brenda Clifton
Director
Volunteer Action Center
Satellite of Cincinnati
2085 A Front Wheel Drive
Vatavia, OH 45103
Phone: (513) 724-6001

Ruth Slater
Director
Volunteer Registry
WHIRE
215 South Walnut Street
Wooster, OH 44691
Phone: (216) 264-9473
Fax: (216) 264-7879

Barbara Lavin
Program Director
Youngstown/Mahoning Valley
Volunteer Center
P.O. Box 46
Youngstown, OH 44501
Phone: (216) 747-5111

OKLAHOMA
State Office:
Holly Drummond
Coordinator
Oklahoma Office of Volunteerism
Office of the Secretary of State
101 State Capitol
Oklahoma City, OK 73105
Phone: (405) 521-3911
Fax: (405) 521-3771

Debra V. Hampton
Community Services Coordinator
Volunteer Center of American Red
    Cross & Tissue Services
601 NE Sixth Street
Oklahoma City, OK 73104
Phone: (405) 232-7121
Fax: (405) 236-5691

Mary L. Finley
Director
Tulsa Volunteer Center
1430 South Boulder
Tulsa, OK 74119
Phone: (918) 585-5551
Fax: (918) 585-3285

OREGON
State Office:
Peggi Timm
State Director
Department of Human Resources
DHR Volunteer Program
500 Summer Street, Fourth Floor
Salem, OR 97310-0308
Phone: (503) 373-1618
Fax: (503) 378-6532

Terry Lake
Director
United Way of Lane County
Voluntary Action Center
123 Oakway Center
Eugene, OR 97401-5666
Phone: (503) 484-6666
Fax: (503) 686-3411

Will L. Wiebe
Director
Volunteer Center
718 West Burnside, Room 404
Portland, OR 97209
Phone: (503) 222-1355

PENNSYLVANIA
State Office:
John A. Briscoe
Director
PennSERVE: Governor's Office of
    Citizen Involvement
Department of Labor & Industry
1304 Labor and Industry Building
Harrisburg, PA 17120
Phone: (717) 787-1971
Fax: (717) 787-9458

Louise B. Elkins
Associate Director
United Way SEPA Volunteer Centers
Neumann College Life Center
Aston, PA 19014
Phone: (215) 456-2937

Priscilla B. Schueck
Co-Director
Volunteer Center of United Way
2200 Avenue A, Suite 301
Bethlehem, PA 18017-2157
Phone: (215) 691-6670
Fax: (215) 865-5871

Donna B. Cummings
Manager
GUIDELINE
520 Ruah Street

P.O. Box 8
Blossburg, PA 16912
Phone: 1-800-332-6718

Barrie Ann George
Director
Carlisle Volunteer Connection
United Way of Greater Carlisle Area
117 North Hanover
Carlisle, PA 17013
Phone: (717) 243-4805
Fax: (717) 243-8005

Debbie Liadis
Community Services Supervisor
Volunteer Center of
    Clearfield County
P.O. Box 550
Clearfield, PA 16830
Phone: (814) 765-1398
Fax: (814) 765-2760

Nancy Lydic Rogers
Vice President
Volunteer Services Division
United Way of Erie County
110 West Tenth Street
Erie, PA 16501-1466
Phone: (814) 456-2937
Fax: (814) 456-5750

Cheryl Deitz
Director
Volunteer Center
546 Maclay Street
Harrisburg, PA 17110
Phone: (717) 238-6678

Sally Allison
Director
United Way Volunteer Center
630 Janet Avenue
Lancaster, PA 17601
Phone: (717) 299-3743
Fax: (717) 394-6118

Clifton D. Eshbach
Director
Volunteer Center of Lebanon County

Hamilton Bank Building,
801 Cumberland Street
P.O. Box 1164
Lebanon, PA 17042-1164
Phone: (717) 274-9784
Fax: (717) 274-3580

Priscilla B. Schueck
Director
United Way
Voluntary Action Center
P.O. Box 6478
Lehigh Valley, PA 18001-6478
Phone: (215) 758-8010

Mary Wiest Mackie
Director
United Way of SEPA
Volunteer Centers
Seven Benjamin Franklin Parkway
Philadelphia, PA 19103
Phone: (215) 665-2474
Fax: (215) 665-2531

Lavera S. Brown
Director
Volunteer Action Center
United Way of Allegheny County
P.O. Box 735
Pittsburgh, PA 15230-0735
Phone: (412) 456-6880
Fax: (412) 394-3507

Mary Pennington
Director
Volunteer Action Center
JCCEOA, Inc.
Mill Creek Center
105 Grace Way
Punxsutawney, PA 15767-1209
Phone: (814) 938-3302

Monica Ruano-Wenrich
Volunteer Services Manager
Volunteer Center
United Way of Berks County, Inc.
501 Washington Street
P.O. Box 302

Reading, PA 19603-0302
Phone: (215) 371-4571
Fax: (215) 371-4569

James Gallagher
Director
Voluntary Action Center of
  Northeast Pennsylvania
225 North Washington Avenue
Scranton, PA 18503
Phone: (717) 347-5616
Fax: (717) 341-5816

Joan Wheatcroft
Volunteer Coordinator
Information & Referral Center
OHR, Box 396
Selinsgrove, PA 17870

Marie Hamilton
Executive Director
Voluntary Action Center of
  Centre County, Inc.
1524 West College Avenue, #8
State College, PA 16801
Phone: (814) 234-8222
Fax: (814) 865-5241

Sandra L. Sabbot
Director
Volunteer Resource Center
United Way of Washington County
58 East Cherry Avenue
Washington, PA 15301
Phone: (412) 225-3310
Fax: (412) 225-3322

Carol S. Clegg
Director
Volunteer Action Center of
  Wyoming Valley
United Way of Wyoming Valley
9 East Market Street
Wilkes-Barre, PA 18711-0351
Phone: (717) 822-3020
Fax: (717) 822-0522

Lisa Johnson
Director
Volunteer Center of York County
United Way Building
800 E. King Street
York, PA 17403
Phone: (717) 846-4477

RHODE ISLAND
State Office:
Lezlee Shaffer
Director
Volunteers in Action, Inc.
168 Broad Street
Providence, RI 02903-4061
Phone: (401) 421-6547

SOUTH CAROLINA
State Office:
Diane Coleman
Volunteer Services Liaison
Office of the Governor
1205 Pendleton Street
Columbia, SC 29201
Phone: (803) 734-0398
Fax: (803) 734-0385

Terri Gowdy
Director
Western Foothills United Way
  Volunteer Center
114 West Greenville Street
Anderson, SC 29622
Phone: (803) 226-3438
Fax: (803) 226-3430

David Hislop
Executive Director
Volunteer & Information Center of
  Beaufort
P.O. Box 202
Beaufort, SC 29901-0202
Phone: (803) 524-4357
Fax: (803) 524-1915

Leslie S. Davis
Director
Voluntary Action Center
P.O. Box 20696
Charleston, SC 29413-0696
Phone: (803) 723-5000
Fax: (803) 720-2782

Myra Blackman
Director
Voluntary Action Center
United Way of the Midlands
P.O. Box 152
Columbia, SC 29202
Phone: (803) 733-5400
Fax: (803) 779-7803

Nancy Maloney
Director
Volunteer Greenville—
   A Volunteer Center
301 University Ridge, Suite 5300
Greenville, SC 29601-3672
Phone: (803) 232-6444
Fax: (803) 240-8535

Shannon G. Balentine
Director
Volunteer Greenwood
P.O. Box 295
Greenwood, SC 29648
Phone: (803) 229-4103

Linda Silver
Director
Volunteer Center of Hilton Head
20 Palmetto Parkway, Suite 106
Hilton Head Island, SC 29926
Phone: (803) 681-7811
Fax: (803) 681-7821

Elizabeth S. Fisher
Director
Oconee Volunteer & Information
   Services—OVIS
P.O. Box 1828
Seneca, SC 29679-1828

Phone: (803) 882-8899
Fax: (803) 882-8899

Kristina Berry
Director
United Way of the Piedmont
Volunteer Center
101 West St. John Street
   Suite 307
Spartanburg, SC 29304
Phone: (803) 582-7556
Fax: (803) 582-9826

Joann M. Morris
Director
Volunteer Sumter
P.O. Box 957
Sumter, SC 29151
Phone: (803) 775-9424

SOUTH DAKOTA
State Office:
Kersten Johnson
Special Assistant to the Governor
   for Volunteerism
Governor's Office
500 East Capitol Avenue
Pierre, SD 57501-5070
Phone: (605) 773-3661
Fax: (605) 773-4711

Elaine Larson
Director
Volunteer & Information Center
3011 South Phillips Avenue
Sioux Falls, SD 57105
Phone: (605) 334-6646

Pam Kettering
Director
Yankton Volunteer & Information
   Center
P.O. Box 387
Yankton, SD 57078
Phone: (605) 665-6067

TENNESSEE
State Office:
Jim Hall
Director of State Planning
Tennessee Department of
    Human Services
Governor's Office
State Capitol, G-12
Nashville, TN 37219
Phone: (615) 741-4131
Fax: (615) 741-1416

Patricia B. Eaker
Director
Volunteer Center of Chattanooga
P.O. Box 4029
Chattanooga, TN 37405-4029
Phone: (615) 265-0514
Fax: (615) 752-0350

Kathy Hunnell
Volunteer Office Manager
Volunteer Clearing House of
    Bradley County
4410 Urbane Road
Cleveland, TN 37312
Phone: (615) 479-1196

Debbie White
Director
Volunteer ETSU
East Tennessee State University
P.O. Box 70618
Johnson City, TN 37614
Phone: (615) 929-5675
Fax: (615) 929-6825

Carol Sloan
Executive Director
Volunteer Johnson City, Inc.
P.O. Box 1443
Johnson City, TN 37605-1443
Phone: (615) 926-8010
Fax: (615) 928-8437

Mary Ann Morie
Director
Volunteer Kingsport, Inc.

1701 Virginia Avenue, Suite 17
Kingsport, TN 37664
Phone: (615) 247-4511

Donna Deichert
Director
Volunteer Center
United Way of Knoxville
P.O. Box 326
Knoxville, TN 37901-0326
Phone: (615) 523-9131
Fax: (615) 522-7312

Elizabeth S. Duncan
Director
Volunteer Center of Memphis
1698 Monroe Avenue
Memphis, TN 38104
Phone: (901) 276-8655
Fax: (901) 276-6953

Judy Hough
Volunteer Services Specialist
Volunteer Center
United Way of Middle Tennessee
250 Venture Circle
Nashville, TN 37228
Phone: (615) 256-8272
Fax: (615) 780-2426

TEXAS
State Office:
Cynthia Galvin
Director
Governor's Office of Community
    Leadership/Volunteer Services
P.O. Box 12428
Austin, TX 78711
Phone: (512) 463-1782
Fax: (512) 463-1849

Angel Whiteside
Director
Volunteer Center of Abilene, Inc.
P.O. Box 3953
Abilene, TX 79604
Phone: (915) 676-5683
Fax: (915) 673-5520

Jill Marufo
Coordinator
United Way Volunteer Action Center
2211 Line Avenue
Amarillo, TX 79106
Phone: (806) 376-6714
Fax: (806) 376-9343

Becky Hagena Solis
Director
Volunteer Resource Center
P.O. Box 1959
Angleton, TX 77516
Phone: (409) 849-4404
Fax: (409) 848-0259

Debbi McCall
Assistant Director
Volunteer Center, Southeast
    Metropolitan Tarrant County
401 West Sanford
Arlington, TX 76011
Phone: (817) 860-1613
Fax: (817) 277-6919

Ryan Robertson
Director
Capital Area Volunteer Center, Inc.
3409 Executive Center Drive, Suite 23
Austin, TX 78731
Phone: (512) 346-1313
Fax: (512) 346-1161

Betsy Boyt
Director
Volunteer Action Center of
    Southeast Texas
P.O. Box 2945
Beaumont, TX 77704
Phone: (409) 832-3290

Sandra Alson
Director
Volunteer Center—Northeast
813 Browntrail
Bedford, TX 76022-7338
Phone: (817) 282-0970
Fax: (817) 282-1275

Gilna Nance
Director
Volunteer Center of the Coastal Bend
3154 Reid Drive, Suite 202
Corpus Christi, TX 78404-2522
Phone: (512) 855-3500
Fax: (512) 855-3500

Julie Thomas
Director
Volunteer Center of Dallas County
1215 Skiles
Dallas, TX 75204
Phone: (214) 826-6767
Fax: (214) 821-8716

Ann Goodman
Director (Interim)
Volunteer Bureau of United Way of
    El Paso
P.O. Box 3488
El Paso, TX 79923
Phone: (915) 532-4919
Fax: (915) 533-7921

Nancy K. Saenz
Director
Volunteer Center of Metropolitan
    Tarrant County
210 East Ninth Street
Fort Worth, TX 76402-6494
Phone: (817) 878-0099
Fax: (817) 878-0092

Carrie Moffitt
Executive Director
Volunteer Center of
    the Texas Gulf Coast
3100 Timmons Lane, Suite 100
Houston, TX 77027
Phone: (713) 965-0031
Fax: (713) 965-9602

Jean Humphrey
Coordinator
Volunteer Center of Longview
P.O. Box 3443
Longview, TX 75606

Phone: (903) 758-2374
Fax: (903) 753-8419

Louise Cummins
Director
Volunteer Center of Lubbock
1706 23rd Street, Suite 101
Lubbock, TX 79411-1214
Phone: (806) 747-0551
Fax: (806) 747-8640

Natalie West
Director
Volunteer Resource Center, Inc.
2213 Primrose
McAllen, TX 78504
Phone: (512) 630-3003

Laura Walker
Director (Interim)
Volunteer Center of Midland
1031 Andrews Highway, Suite 210
Midland, TX 79701
Phone: (915) 520-3108
Fax: (915) 697-8781

Mary Jo Dean
Director
Volunteer Center of Plano
301 W. Parker Road, Suite 213
Plano, TX 75023
Phone: (214) 422-1050
Fax: (214) 578-9369

Sallie Peacock
Director
United Way of San Antonio &
    Bexar Counties
P.O. Box 898
San Antonio, TX 78293-0898
Phone: (512) 224-5000
Fax: (512) 224-4245

Marie Benson
Director
Texarkana Volunteer Center
3000 Texas Boulevard
Texarkana, TX 75503

Phone: (903) 793-4903

Rebecca Wade
Director
Volunteer Center of Tyler
113 East Houston
Tyler, TX 75702
Phone: (903) 592-6342
Fax: (903) 592-6342

Dorothy Wienecke
Director
Volunteer Connection
P.O. Box 2027
Community Services Building
201 W. Waco Drive
Waco, TX 76703
Phone: (817) 753-5683
Fax: (817) 753-5789

UTAH
Chris Smith
Director
Voluntary Action Center
236 North, 100 East
P.O. Box 567
Logan, UT 84321-0567
Phone: (801) 752-3103

Leann PoVey Jackson
Director
Volunteer Center
2650 Lincoln, Suite 331
Ogden, UT 84401
Phone: (801) 635-3777
Fax: (801) 625-3690

Liela Lavaki
Director
United Way Volunteer Center
P.O. Box 135
148 N. 100 West
Provo, UT 84603
Phone: (801) 374-8108
Fax: (801) 374-2591

Rita Inoway
Director

Volunteer Center
212 West 1300 South
Salt Lake City, UT 84115
Phone: (801) 486-2136
Fax: (801) 486-2140

VIRGINIA
State Office:
Beth Hayes
Director
Virginia Office of Volunteerism
223 Governor Street
Richmond, VA 23219
Phone: (804) 786-1431
Fax: (804) 371-8654

Mary LaMois
Director
Alexandria Volunteer Bureau
801 North Pitt Street, Suite 102
Alexandria, VA 22314
Phone: (703) 836-2176

Jean Berg
Director
Arlington County Volunteer Office
2100 Clarendon Boulevard, Suite 314
Arlington, VA 22201
Phone: (703) 358-3222
Fax: (703) 358-3295

Alison Limoges
Director
Volunteer Action Center of
    Montgomery County, Inc.
P.O. Box 565
Blacksburg, VA 24063-0565
Phone: (703) 552-4909

Margaret Herrin
Director
Volunteer-Bristol
600 Cumberland Street,
    Second Floor
Bristol, VA 24201
Phone: (703) 669-1555

Diana Wallace
Director

Appalachian Agency
Senior Citizens South
P.O. Box 765
Cedar Bluff, VA 24609
Phone: (703) 964-4915
Fax: (703) 963-0130

Cherry D. Rubio
Director
United Way Volunteer Center
413 East Market, Suite 101
Charlottesville, VA 22902
Phone: (804) 972-1705
Fax: (804) 972-1719

Ruth M. Meier
Executive Director
Voluntary Action Center of Fairfax
    County Area, Inc.
10530 Page Avenue
Fairfax, VA 22030
Phone: (703) 246-3460

Kimberly Smart
Director
Rappahannock Volunteer Connection
P.O. Box 398
Fredericksburg, VA 22404
Phone: (703) 373-0041
Fax: (703) 373-0356

Elyse Brown
Director
Voluntary Action Center of the
    United Way
P.O. Box 9007
Hampton, VA 23670
Phone: (804) 838-9770
Fax: (804) 838-5930

Marilyn Blake
Director
Volunteer Services of Hanover
    County
P.O. Box 470
Hanover, VA 23069
Phone: (804) 798-0896
Fax: (804) 798-6212

Marilyn Dunnill
Executive Director
Loudoun Volunteer Center
30B Catoctin Circle SE
Leesburg, VA 22075
Phone: (703) 777-0113
Fax: (703) 771-5844

Sandra Brooks
Director
Voluntary Action Center of United
    Way of Central Virginia
1010 Miller Park Square
Lynchburg, VA 24501
Phone: (804) 847-8657
Fax: (804) 847-8753

Pauline Frank
Director
Voluntary Action Center of
    the Prince William Area
9300 Peabody Street, Suite 108
Manassas, VA 22110
Phone: (703) 369-5292

The Volunteer Connection of
    South Hampton
100 E. Main Street
Norfolk, VA 23510
Phone: (804) 624-2403

Jane Fleming
Director
Volunteers in Service
Norton Department of Public Welfare
P.O. Box 378
Norton, VA 24273
Phone: (703) 679-2701
Fax: (703) 679-0607

Timothy P. Holtz
Director
Volunteer Resources Association
United Way Services
P.O. Box 227
Petersburg, VA 23804
Phone: (804) 861-9330

Jennie Sue Murdock
President
Voluntary Action Center of
    Roanoke Valley
P.O. Box 598
Roanoke, VA 24004
Phone: (703) 985-0131
Fax: (703) 982-2935

Janet P. Pregram
Director
Volunteer Center of
    United Way Services
224 East Broad Street
P.O. Box 12209
Richmond, VA 23241
Phone: (804) 771-5851
Fax: (804) 225-7344

Doris Perry
Director
Suffolk Voluntary Action
    Information & Referral Center
350 North Main Street
P.O. Box 452
Suffolk, VA 23434
Phone: (804) 539-0316

Carolyn Kincaid
Director
Volunteer Connection
United Way of Greater
    Williamsburg
109 Cary Street
Williamsburg, VA 23185
Phone: (804) 229-2222
Fax: (804) 253-2837

Linda Caley
Director
Volunteer Center for United Way
    Northern Shenandoah
212 S. Braddock Street
P.O. Box 460
Winchester, VA 22601
Phone: (703) 662-9366

VERMONT
State Offices:
Jane Williams
Special Assistant
Governor's Commission on
    Volunteerism
109 State Street
Montpelier, VT 05609
Phone: (802) 828-3333
Fax: (802) 828-3339

Carol Todd
Chair
Vermont Governor's Commission
    on Volunteers
63 Central Street
Northfield, VT 05663
Phone: (802) 828-8803
Fax: (802) 828-8855

Dolly Fleming
Director
Volunteer Connection
United Way of Chittendon County
95 St. Paul Street
Burlington, VT 05401
Phone: (802) 864-7498
Fax: (802) 864-7401

WASHINGTON
State Office:
Joby Winans
Administrator
Center for Volunteerism and
    Citizen Service
906 Columbia Street SW
P.O. Box 48300
Olympia, WA 98504-8300
Phone: (206) 786-8207
Fax: (206) 586-5880

Ruth Eklund
Executive Director
RSVP Volunteer Center
411 York Street
Bellingham, WA 98225

Phone: (206) 734-3055
Fax: (206) 734-3215

Evelyn Edeen
Administrative Assistant
United Way of Snohomish County
Volunteer Center
917 134th Street SW, A-6
Everett, WA 98204
Phone: (206) 742-5911
Fax: (206) 743-1440

Hazel Batchelor
Director
Benton-Franklin Volunteer Center
10 North Washington, Suite 4
Kennewick, WA 99336
Phone: (509) 582-0631

Sandy Evrest
Coordinator
Voluntary Action Center
Skagit County Community
    Action Agency
613 South Second
Mt. Vernon, WA 98273
Phone: (206) 336-6627
Fax: (206) 336-9771

Richard Hinkle
Director (Interim)
Volunteer Center of
    Thurston County
2618 12th Court SW
Olympia, WA 98502
Phone: (206) 786-8207

Kris Kero
Director
United Way Volunteer Center of
    King County
107 Cherry Street, 7th Floor
Seattle, WA 98104
Phone: (206) 461-4539
Fax: (206) 461-8453

Jacqueline Ferrell-Fleury
Coordinator

United Way's Volunteer Center
P.O. Box 326
Spokane, WA 99210-0326
Phone: (509) 624-2279
Fax: (509) 624-0840

Nina Ruch
Coordinator
Helpline Association
United Way of Pierce County
734 Broadway
Tacoma, WA 98401
Phone: (206) 272-4267
Fax: (206) 597-7481

Anne Turner
Director
Volunteer Bureau of Clark County
P.O. Box 425
Vancouver, WA 98666-0425
Phone: (206) 694-6577
Fax: (206) 694-6716

Renée Kabrich
Director
Greater Yakima Volunteer Center
302 West Lincoln
Yakima, WA 98902
Phone: (509) 248-4460
Fax: (509) 457-7897

WEST VIRGINIA
Betty Hopkins
Director
Volunteer Action Center
P.O. Box 777
Parkersburg, WV 26102
Phone: (304) 422-8505

WISCONSIN
Mark Germano
Executive Director
Information & Referral Center
120 N. Morrison Street
Appleton, WI 54911
Phone: (414) 739-5126
Fax: (414) 739-2945

Nancy Boutelle
Director
Voluntary Action Center
431 Olympian Boulevard
Beloit, WI 53511
Phone: (608) 365-1278
Fax: (608) 365-1432

Connie Kopaczewski
Director
Chippewa Valley Volunteer Center
316 Eau Claire Street
Eau Claire, WI 54701
Phone: (715) 832-3903

Christine Danielson
Director
Volunteer Center
338 South Chestnut
Green Bay, WI 54303-1530
Phone: (414) 435-1101

Gloria Ramirez
Executive Director
Voluntary Action Center of
  Kenosha, Inc.
716 58th Street
Kenosha, WI 53140
Phone: (414) 657-4554
Fax: (414) 654-2194

Kathy Martinson
Director
Voluntary Action Center
United Way of Dane County
P.O. Box 7548
Madison, WI 53707
Phone: (608) 246-4380
Fax: (608) 246-4349

Cheri Farnsworth
Director
Volunteer County of Ozaukee County
14135 North Cedarburg Road
Mequon, WI 53092
Phone: (414) 377-1616

Becky Turner
Director

Volunteer Center of
Greater Milwaukee
600 E. Mason Street, Suite 100
Milwaukee, WI 53202
Phone: (414) 273-7887
Fax: (414) 273-0637

Pamela Zabrowski
Executive Director
Volunteer Center of Wuakesha
County, Inc.
2220 Silvernail Road
Prewaukee, WI 53072
Phone: (414) 544-0150

Mary Mahr
Director
Volunteer Center of Portage County
1045 Clark Street, Suite 204
Stevens Point, WI 54481
Phone: (715) 341-6740

Maria Maher
Executive Director
Volunteer Center of
Marathon County
407 Grant Street
City Hall
Wausau, WI 54401
Phone: (715) 843-1220

Rita M. Sorensen
Director
Volunteer Center of
Washington County
120 North Main Street, Suite 340
West Bend, WI 53095
Phone: (414) 338-8256
Fax: (414) 334-5402

Volunteer Center of
South Wood County
1120 Lincoln Street, Suite 2
Wisconsin Rapids, WI 54494
Phone: (715) 421-0390
Fax: (715) 423-1865

WYOMING
State Office:
John Freeman
Director
Wyoming Volunteer Assistance
Corporation
c/o Wyoming Centennial
Community Federation
P.O. Box 4008, University Station
Laramie, WY 82071
Phone: (307) 766-2477

Mary A. Schwem
Director
Volunteer Information Center
P.O. Box 404
Cheyenne, WY 82003
Phone: (307) 632-4132

CANADA
Janet Lautenschlager
Senior Program Officer
Voluntary Action Directorate
Department of the Secretary of
State of Canada
Ottowa, Ont. K1A 0M5
CANADA
Phone: (819) 994-2255
Fax: (819) 953-4131

Volunteer Ontario
2 Dunbloor Road, Suite 203
Etobicoke, Ont. M9A 2E4
CANADA
Phone: (416) 236-0588
Fax: (416) 487-6150

Kingston Community
Volunteer Bureau
23 Carlisle Street
Kingston, Ont. K7K 3X1
CANADA
Phone: (613) 542-8512

Thelma Roy
Director

Moncton Volunteer Centre
Du Benevolat
236 St. George Street, Suite 406
Moncton, N.B. E1C 1W1
CANADA
Phone: (506) 857-8005

Leslie MacLean
Director
Saint John Volunteer Centre
P.O. Box 7091, Station A
Saint John, N.B. E2L 4S5
CANADA
Phone: (506) 658-1555
Fax: (506) 633-7724

PUERTO RICO
Maribel Rodriguez-Ema
Director
Voluntarios por Puerto Rico
P.O. Box 1914
Hato Rey, PR 00919-1914
Phone: (809) 728-7099

2

National Volunteer Opportunities

THIS IS A LIST OF NATIONAL ORGANIZATIONS with local chapters that link volunteers with people in need. Special thanks to Noble Press, Inc. for permission to use annotated agency references in David E. Driver's *The Good Heart Book* (1989). These agencies are marked with an asterisk (*).

* ACTION
Purpose: Federal Domestic Volunteer Agency. Supports, promotes and recognizes voluntarism in America.

Programs include Foster Grandparent Program, Young Volunteers in Action, Senior Companion Program, Volunteer Drug Use Prevention Program, and more.

Volunteer needs vary according to program and location. One example: the Foster Grandparent program matches companions with children who have special or exceptional needs, such as physical handicaps or a history of abuse or neglect.

For more information on volunteering, contact:
ACTION
National Headquarters
Washington, D.C. 20525
Phone:1-800-424-8580

* American Association of Retired Persons (AARP)
Purpose: To enhance the quality of life for older persons; to promote independence, dignity and purpose for older persons; to lead in determining the role and place of older persons in society, and to improve the image of aging.

Volunteers are used as policymakers, advisors, educators, advocates, and providers of support and assistance in AARP programs.

For more information, contact:
American Association of Retired Persons
National Headquarters
1909 K Street NW
Washington, D.C. 20049
Phone:(202) 434-2277

* Association of Retarded Citizens (ARC)

Mission: Dedicated to improving the quality of life of people with mental retardation, preventing this disabling condition, and searching for cures.

Their programs serve retarded citizens in the areas of education, job training and placement, independent living and personal fulfillment. Also, there are programs to assist families, organizations and communities in meeting the needs of people with mental retardation.

Volunteers are needed to get involved in citizen advocacy programs, recreational activities, public education, employment programs, etc.

This is a national organization. *The best way to volunteer is to call your local ARC office or contact:*
Association of Retarded Citizens
National Headquarters
500 E. Border, Suite 300
Arlington, TX 76010
Phone:1-800-433-5255

* Big Brothers and Big Sisters of America

Services: Professionally supervised friendships between a mature adult and a child who benefits from the guidance and examples set by the adult.

Concerned, responsible men and women are needed to volunteer to serve as Big Brothers and Big Sisters, speakers, etc.

This is a national organization. *Volunteer in your local community or contact the national headquarters for more information:*
Big Brothers and Big Sisters of America
National Headquarters
230 N. 13th Street
Philadelphia, PA 19107
Phone: (215) 567-7000

*Boys and Girls Clubs of America

Purpose: Boys and Girls Clubs work to help youth of all backgrounds, with special concern for those from disadvantaged circumstances, develop the qualities needed to become responsible citizens and leaders. Services include career exploration, health and physical fitness, delinquency prevention, citizen and leadership development, etc.

Volunteer needs vary with each club or organization. May include coaching, tutoring, art/crafts instruction, career guidance, board support, etc.

This is a national organization. *For more information about volunteer opportunities, check your local phone book or call:*

Boys Clubs of America
National Headquarters
771 First Avenue
New York, NY 10017
Phone: (212) 351-5900

* Catholic Charities USA

Purpose: Serves those in need, advocates for the poor, and works with others for peace and justice.

Catholic Charities USA provides leadership and support to its members, who offer numerous services to their communities, ranging from adoption and substance abuse counseling to help for the hungry and homeless.

While not every local Catholic Charities agency is set up to use volunteers, many rely on volunteers for a variety of services. *For more information contact:*

Catholic Charities USA
National Headquarters
1731 King Street, Suite 200
Alexandria, VA 22314
Phone: (703) 549-1390

Compeer, Inc.

Mission: To provide Compeer service to people who have developmental disabilities such as mental retardation or autism.

Compeer ("noun which means equal or peer") volunteers have direct contact with the person being helped. They commit to spending at least one hour a week for a year with a person who has a mental illness. They do things friends would do together: shopping, having dinner, etc. There is ongoing professional support for the volunteer. Compeers soon lose their fears and learn that people who have been labeled as "disabled" are really normal people who face unusual challenges.

This is a national organization operating in several states. *The best way to volunteer is to contact the national office:*

COMPEER, Inc.
259 Monroe Avenue, Suite B-1
Rochester, New York 14607
Phone: (716) 546-8280

*Family Service America
Purpose: Dedicated to strengthening the family.

Family Service America provides a variety of family-related services, including marital counseling, crisis intervention, substance abuse counseling, and more.

Member agencies may use volunteers in community education, direct service (such as drivers), or friendly visitors, etc.

This is a national organization. *For information on volunteer opportunities contact:*
Family Service America
National Headquarters
11700 W. Lake Park Drive
Milwaukee, WI 53224
Phone: (414) 359-1040

* Girl Scouts of the USA
Purpose: Gives girls from all segments of America life a chance to develop their potential to make friends and become a vital part of their community. Based on ethical values, youths work in partnership with adult volunteers.

A continuing adventure in learning that offers a broad range of activities which address the girls' current interests and future roles. Stimulates self-discovery. They are introduced to the worlds of science, the arts, the outdoors, and people.

Volunteers are used as leaders, consultants, board members, staff specialists in child development, administrators, educators, etc.

Contact your local organization or call:
Girl Scouts of the USA
National Headquarters
420 5th Avenue
New York, New York 10018-2702
Phone: (212) 852-8000

* Goodwill Industries of America
Purpose: Provides opportunities for people with disabilities or other hardships to live and work to their fullest potential.

Individual Goodwill offices run a variety of programs, which may include vocational guidance, rehabilitation counseling, socialization activities, and more.

Volunteer needs vary at each independently run office, but common positions include friendly visitors, counselors, day care assistants, etc.

This is a national organization. *For more information, contact:*
Goodwill Industries of America
9200 Wisconsin Avenue
Bethesda, MD 20814
Phone: (301) 530-6500

* Habitat for Humanity
Purpose: Dedicated to providing "a decent house in a decent community for God's people in need."

Habitat builds homes by enlisting donations for materials and volunteers to work on all aspects of building or renovating a house.

Volunteers work in all aspects of construction—carpentry, painting, plumbing. Also administrative support, accounting, public speaking, and other positions related to the promotion of public awareness.

This is a national organization. *For more information on volunteer - ing, contact:*
Habitat for Humanity
National Headquarters
121 Habitat Street
Americus, GA 31709-3498

Hospice
Mission: To provide support services to families who choose to keep their terminally ill family member at home.

There is opportunity for volunteers to have personal contact with the individuals served. They provide respite care, transportation, and befriend and support the terminally ill person and his or her family. Volunteers receive special training in many areas, including the grieving process.

This is a national organization. *The best way to volunteer is to call a local Hospice office or call the national hotline:*
Hospice
1901 N. Moore Street, Suite 901
Arlington, VA 22209
1-800-658-8898

* Laubach Literacy International
Purpose: To reduce illiteracy using volunteer tutors in a one-to-one teaching environment.

Laubach Literacy International recruits and trains volunteers, seeks out individuals who need to improve basic reading and writing skills, and coordinates tutoring match-ups. In addition, they work to promote public awareness about the problems of illiteracy.

Volunteers are needed as tutors, tutor trainers, fundraisers, advisory board members, child care helpers, drivers, clerical assistants, etc.

For more information on volunteer opportunities and locations, contact:
Laubach Literacy International
National Headquarters
1320 Jamesville
Syracuse, NY 13210
Phone: (315) 422-9121

* Literacy Volunteers of America

Purpose: To recruit and train volunteers, seek out individuals who need to improve basic reading and writing skills, and coordinate tutoring matchups. In addition, they work to promote public awareness about the problems of illiteracy.

Volunteers are used as tutors, tutor trainers, fundraisers, advisory board members, child care helpers, drivers, clerical assistants, etc.

For more information, contact:
Literacy Volunteers of America
National Headquarters
5795 Widewaters Parkway
Syracuse, NY
Phone: (315) 445-8000

LOVE INC, A Ministry of World Vision

Mission: To link church volunteers from many different denominations with people at their point of need through a LOVE INC clearinghouse.

LOVE INC (In the Name of Christ) uses volunteers in every area of ministry. Needs come into the clearinghouse and a trained person analyzes the need to make sure it is specific, manageable, and legitimate. The person in need is then directed to a local church which maintains a "talent bank" of volunteers. Linkage is made between a church volunteer with appropriate skills or with an existing agency which meets the need in the community. Volunteers are trained at all levels. There is cooperation between churches and agencies so there is no duplication of services.

This is a national clearinghouse ministry. *The best way to volunteer or inquire about starting a clearinghouse in your community is to contact:*

LOVE INC/World Vision
919 W. Huntington Dr.
Monrovia, CA 91016
Phone: (818) 305-7815

* Lutheran Volunteer Corps
Purpose: A ministry of Luther Place Memorial Church in Washington, D.C.

LVC volunteers work in a variety of urban social justice and human care agencies such as homeless shelters, neighborhood centers, and peace and justice organizations. Agencies are located in five cities across the country.

Volunteer positions range from direct service to advocacy to policy making. A full-time, one-year commitment is required. Volunteers receive orientation, placement, job training, housing, a subsistence salary, and medical insurance.

For more information, contact:
Lutheran Volunteer Corps
National Headquarters
1226 Vermont Avenue NW
Washington, D.C. 20005
Phone: (202) 387-3222

* National Committe for Prevention of Child Abuse
Purpose: Dedicated to involving all concerned citizens in actions to prevent child abuse.

The national office and local chapters administer programs which address a variety of issues, including public awareness, public education, advocacy, and community-based prevention services.

This volunteer-based organization needs individuals to work in community level programs and help implement new programs, or to serve on the national volunteer board of directors.

For more information, contact:
National Committee for Prevention of Child Abuse
332 South Michigan Avenue, Suite 1600
Chicago, IL 60604
Phone: (312) 663-3520

* National Coalition for the Homeless
Purpose: Research and advocacy for the rights of the homeless.

Supports legislation to improve and provide shelters, assists and advises shelters throughout the country, serves as a central source of information and referral on matters pertaining to homelessness.

Volunteers are advocates, speakers, shelter workers, etc.

For information about this national organization, contact:
National Coalition for the Homeless
National Headquarters
1612 K Street NW, #1004
Washington, D.C. 20006
Phone: (202) 775-1322

* National Easter Seal Society
Purpose: Provide direct services to meet rehabilitation needs of persons with disabilities, thereby increasing their self-sufficiency and independence.

Direct services include physical, occupational, and speech language therapies, vocational evaluation and training, camping and recreation, counseling, screening, family support, advocacy, etc.

Volunteers are needed in several areas listed above. Also, drivers for clients, office workers, camp helpers, etc.

For information, contact:
National Easter Seal Society
National Headquarters
70 E. Lake Street
Chicago, IL 60601
Phone: (312) 726-6200

National Federation of Interfaith Volunteer Caregivers, Inc.
Mission: Seeks to strengthen and expand the ministry of caregiving throughout the nation.

This organization seeks to assist congregations of all faiths to undertake the ministry of caregiving to disabled persons and their families by using volunteers. They offer technical assistance and support.

This is a national organization in many states. *For information on developing a volunteer project or volunteering in your community, contact:*
National Federation of Interfaith Volunteer Caregivers
Kingston Medical Arts Building
368 Broadway, Suite 103
P.O. Box 1939
Kingston, NY 12401
Phone: (914) 331-1358

* National School Volunteer Program
Purpose: Promotes and coordinates volunteer efforts in schools, acts as liaison between community and school system.

Volunteers needed as tutors, teacher's aides, field trip chaperones, and more.

For information on volunteering, contact:
National School Volunteer Program
National Headquarters
701 N. Fairfax Street
Alexandria, VA 22314
Phone: (703) 836-7100

* The National Urban League

Purpose: Supports and promotes equal opportunity for minorities.

Services include housing, job training and placement, research and advocacy for minorities on local, state, and national levels, and more.

Volunteer needs: Advocates, literacy tutors, etc.

For informtion, contact:
The National Urban League
National Headquarters
500 East 62nd Street
New York, NY 10021
Phone: (212) 310-9000

Prison Fellowship

Mission: To exhort and assist the church in its ministry to prisoners, ex-prisoners, victims and their families, and in its advancement of biblical standards of justice.

Volunteers play a vital role in bringing the peace of Christ to those affected by crime. Volunteers bring the gospel to prisoners, ex-prisoners and their families through in-prison seminars, Bible studies, marriage seminars, Angel Tree (a ministry to children of prisoners), mentoring, and after-care programs. Justice Fellowship promotes restorative justice principles and uses volunteer task forces to work for and promote biblical standards of justice. Neighbors Who Care is a program that uses volunteers to provide assistance to victims of property crimes. Prison Fellowship provides special training to its volunteers.

To volunteer, please contact your local office. *The national office is located in Reston, Virginia, and the mailing address is:*
Prison Fellowship
P.O. Box 17500
Washington, D.C. 20041-0500
Phone: (703) 478-0100

* Recording for the Blind

Purpose: Dedicated to assisting students at all academic levels, business or professional people—or anyone with a visual, physical, or perceptual disability that prevents the reading of standard printed material.

They provide recorded educational books free on loan to blind and other print-disabled people throughout the world.

Volunteer Needs: Readers, who must first pass a reading test, and monitors, who follow the text for accuracy and tape the recording sessions. Must have at least two years of college and commit to a minimum number of volunteer hours per week. Training is provided.

For more information, contact:
Recording for the Blind
National Headquarters
20 Roszel Road
Princeton, NJ 08540
Phone: (609) 452-0606

* The Salvation Army

Purpose: Provides a balance of spiritual and physical support to all people in need without distinction as to race or creed and without adherence, simulated or real, to the principles of the Army.

Services include: resident alcohol rehabilitation centers; maternity homes and outpatient services for unwed mothers; emergency disaster services; youth outreach programs; senior citizen programs; and more.

Volunteer needs vary depending on the programs offered in your area. May use tutors, youth counselors and recreation leaders, etc.

For information or to volunteer, contact your local Salvation Army office or the national headquarters at:
The Salvation Army
National Headquarters
615 Slaters Lane
P.O. Box 269
Alexandria, VA 22313
Phone: (703) 684-5500

* United Way of America

Mission: "To increase the organized capacity of people to care for one another."

United Way services include funding and/or administration over human care and social justice agencies (these may be United Way offices, chapters of other nationwide organizations, or one-of-a-kind grassroots organizations founded by people who recognize health and human care needs in their communities); recruiting and training volunteers; and operating many volunteer and voluntary action centers.

This is a national organization. For more information on how and where you can volunteer, contact your local United Way Voluntary Action Center or call the national organization:

United Way of America
National Headquarters
701 N. Fairfax Street
Alexandria, VA 22314
Phone: (703) 836-7100

* Volunteers in Service to America (VISTA)

Purpose: VISTA strives to enable low-income people throughout the United States to improve their own lives and living conditions.

Services: Drug-abuse counseling; literacy training; food distribution; shelters for the homeless; neighborhood revitalization; and more.

Volunteers should be eighteen years or older and be willing to make a full-time, year-long commitment to the VISTA program.

For volunteer opportunities, contact the national headquarters:
Volunteers in Service to America (VISTA)
National Headquarters
111 Vermont NW
Washington, D.C. 20525
Phone: (206) 606-4845

* Volunteers of America

Purpose: Reaching and uplifting of all people in bringing them to the immediate and active service of God. They are sponsored by The Salvation Army.

Their services include operation of low-income residences, homeless shelters, alcohol rehabilitation programs, thrift shops, and more.

Volunteers are used as thrift shop workers, shelter workers, kitchen servers, etc.

This is a national organization. *For information, contact:*
Volunteers of America
National Headquarters
3813 N. Causeway Boulevard
Metairie, LA 70002
Phone: (504) 836-5225

3

National Health Care Opportunities

THIS LIST OF VOLUNTEER OPPORTUNITIES available through the offices of national health care organizations is not exhaustive by any means. It is meant to support the wide range of opportunities that exist in the health care field. I encourage you to consult Alan Luks and Peggy Payne's *The Healing Power of Doing Good*, Fawcett Columbine (New York, 1991) for many other challenges.

People With AIDS Coalition
31 West 26th Street, Fifth Floor
New York, NY 10010
Phone: 1-800-828-3280

American Cancer Society
1599 Clifton Road NE
Atlanta, GA 30329

American Heart Association (AHA)
7320 Greenville Avenue
Dallas, TX 75231
Phone: (214) 373-6300

American Red Cross
431 18th St. NW
Washington, D.C. 20006
Phone: (202) 737-8300

Leukemia Society of America
600 Third Avenue
New York, NY 10016
Phone: (212) 573-8484

March of Dimes Birth Defects Foundation
1275 Mamoroneck Avenue
White Plains, NY 10605
Phone: (914) 997-4444

Muscular Dystrophy Association
3300 East Sunrise Drive
Tucson, AZ 85718
Phone: (602) 529-2000

National Association of the Deaf
814 Thayer Avenue

Silver Spring, MD 20910
Phone: (301) 587-1788 (Voice or TDD)

National Easter Seal Society
70 East Lake Street
Chicago, IL 60601
Phone: (312) 908-6075

National Multiple Sclerosis Society
733 Third Avenue
New York, NY 10017
Phone: (212) 986-3240

National Neurofibromatosis Foundation
141 Fifth Avenue, Suite 7-S
New York, NY 10010
Phone: 1-800-323-7938

National Sudden Infant Death Syndrome Foundation
10500 Little Patuxent Parkway
Suite 400
Columbia, MD 21044
Phone: 1-800-221-7437 (outside of Maryland)
(410) 964-8000 (in Maryland)

Rehabilitation Institute of Chicago (RCI)
Director of Volunteer Services
Rehabilitation Institute of Chicago
345 East Superior Street
Chicago, IL 60611
Phone: (312) 908-6075

Notes

ONE
The New Volunteer

1. David Hollister, Remarks at ten-year Anniversary Celebration of Christian Services/LOVE INC of Greater Lansing, Michigan (October 15, 1992).
2. "At A Time When Needed Most, Giving and Volunteering Is Up in All Categories," *Independent Sector Newsletter* (January, 1991).
3. "Does Psychotherapy Work?" *U.S. News & World Report* (May 24, 1993), 57-65.

TWO
The Hidden Benefits of Helping

1. Allan Luks and Peggy Payne, *The Healing Power of Doing Good* (New York, New York: Fawcett Columbine, 1991).
2. Nancy Ramsey, "How Business Can Help the Schools," *Fortune* (October 12, 1992), 147-57.
3. Eileen Rockefeller Growald and Allan Luks, *American Health Magazine* (March, 1988).
4. Dennis Fiely, "The Healing Power of Doing Good: The Health and Spiritual Benefits of Helping Others," *The Columbus Dispatch* (August 28, 1992).
5. Allan Luks, "Helpers High," *Psychology Today* (October, 1988).
6. David E. Driver, *The Good Heart Book: A Guide to Volunteering* (Chicago, Illinois: Noble Press, 1989), 21.
7. "Worldwide Office Environment Index," Harris Study (October, 1991).
8. Laura Saari, "Time to Share, Motivation: Reaching Out Can Lead to Paying Jobs," *The Orange County Register* (November 24, 1991), L2.
9. Richard Bolles, *What Color Is Your Parachute?* (Berkeley, California: Ten-Speed Press, 1972).

THREE
Looking Beyond the Need to See My Neighbor

1. "The New York Times/CBS News Poll," *The New York Times* (January 20, 1992), A9.
2. Michael Harrington. *The Other America* (New York, New York: McMillan, 1962).
3. Gregg Petersmeyer, White House Briefing on World Vision's LOVE INC ministry (May 4, 1990).
4. Charles H. Kraft, *Christianity and Culture: A Study in Dynamic Biblical Theologizing in Cross-Cultural Perspective* (Maryknoll, New York: Orbis, 1979), 1-3.

SIX
Look before You Leap

1. Sue Vineyard, *Grapevine: Volunteerism's Newsletter* (March/April, 1992), 7.
2. *Grapevine* (November/December, 1991), 4.
3. David E. Driver, *The Good Heart Book: A Guide to Volunteering* (Chicago, Illinois: Noble Press, 1989), based on literacy manual, *Volunteers in Adult Basic Education*.

EIGHT
A Time to Give

1. From *New World Decisions*, as cited in article by Daniel Goleman in the *New York Times*, poll conducted for American Board of Family Practice (January/February, 1989).
2. Daniel Goleman, "Compassion and Comfort in Middle Age," *New York Times*, "Science Times" section (February 6, 1990), 1.
3. George E. Valliant, *The Middle Years: New Psychoanalytic Perspectives*, Yale University Press (December, 1989).
4. R.L. Harris, A.M. Ellicott, and D.S. Holmes, "The Timing of Psychosocial Transitions and Changes in Women's Lives: An Examination of Women Aged 45 to 60," *Journal of Personality and Social Psychology* (1986), Vol. 51, 409-16.
5. R. Michels and R. Auchincloss, "The Impact of Middle Age on Ambitions and Ideals," *The Middle Years: New Psychoanalytic Perspective*, editors, J.M. Oldham and R.S. Liebert (New Haven, Connecticut: Yale University Press), 40-57.
6. Patricia Churgot, "Men's Group Touches Kids, Mobilizes Adults," *The Detroit Free Press* (May 19, 1992).
7. E. Erikson, J. Erikson, and H. Kivniok, *Vital Involvement in Old Age* (New York, New York: W.W. Norton, 1986).
8. Kay Kincl, "Providing for the Poor, Why It's Not Business as Usual," *Contempo* (July, 1992), 11-14.
9. *The National and International Religion Report* (May 20, 1991).

10. Diana Fasanella, "Volunteerism Strengthens Family and Community Ties," *The Non-Profit Times* (January, 1993).
11. Dawn Booker, "Families: Organizations Hope to Revive the Tradition," *The Orange County Register* (November 24, 1991).
12. "Volunteering and Giving Among American Teenagers 14-17 Years of Age," *Independent Sector Newsletter* (April, 1992).
13. Marilyn Smith and Michael J. Havercamp, "'Just Do It!': High Risk Teenagers Help Themselves While Helping Others," *The Journal of Volunteer Administration* (Summer, 1991), 4-10.

NINE
Avoiding the Potholes

1. Billy Graham, interview by Diane Sawyer, "A Lion in Winter," *Prime Time Live* (ABC TV) (December 17, 1992).

TEN
When Enough is Enough

1. Jessica Mitford, *Kind and Usual Punishment* (New York, New York: Alfred A. Knopf, 1973), 29.

ELEVEN
Pioneering a Dream

1. Stan Mooneyham, *Dancing on the Strait and Narrow* (San Francisco: Harper & Row, 1960), 24.
2. Brian O'Connell, editor, *America's Voluntary Spirit* (New York: Foundation Center, 1983), foreword by John Gardner.
3. John Burdick, "Unsung Heroes Keep People Off the Bottle," *The Holland Sunday Sentinel* (November 25, 1990).

Another Book of Interest from Servant Publications

Me, Myself & I
*How Far Should We Go in Our
Search for Self-Fulfillment?*

Dr. Archibald Hart

Psychology bashing and twelve-step groups are both on the rise. And Christians are arguing about who or what has the answers to our problems: the Bible or psychology?

As a psychologist and a Christian, Archibald Hart believes it's time to take a searching look at what modern psychology *and* the Bible say about such topics as self-concept, self-image, self-esteem, self-denial, self-sacrifice, and self-surrender. Surely there is a way through these tangled issues that can bring greater clarity to our search for healing.

Me, Myself, & I is a practical handbook for anyone who struggles to understand themselves and others. *$10.99*

Available at your Christian bookstore or from:
**Servant Publications • Dept. 209 • P.O. Box 7455
Ann Arbor, Michigan 48107**
Please include payment plus $1.25 per book
for postage and handling.
*Send for our FREE catalog of Christian
books, music, and cassettes.*